SEAN CONNERY

Robert Tanitch

CHAPMANS

FOR PAM AND BILL JACKSON

Also by Robert Tanitch

A PICTORIAL COMPANION TO SHAKESPEARE'S PLAYS
RALPH RICHARDSON, A TRIBUTE
OLIVIER
LEONARD ROSSITER
ASHCROFT
GIELGUD
DIRK BOGARDE
GUINNESS
JOHN MILLS

Frontispiece: Sean Connery in *The Name of the Rose*

Chapmans Publishers
A division of the Orion Publishing Group Ltd
Orion House
5 Upper St Martin's Lane
London
WC2H 9EA

ISBN 1 85592 665 2

First published by Chapmans 1992
This paperback edition published by Chapmans 1993

Copyright © Robert Tanitch 1992

The right of Robert Tanitch to be identified
as the author of this work has been asserted by
him in accordance with the Copyright,
Designs and Patents Act 1988.

Designed by Judy Linard

Typeset by Monoset Typesetters, London
Printed and bound in Great Britain by
Butler & Tanner Ltd, Frome and London

SEAN
CONNERY

CONTENTS

INTRODUCTION

Sean Connery is acknowledged to be one of the great movie stars and one of the great screen actors of the twentieth century, a legend in his lifetime. This book is a pictorial record and chronology of his career in film, theatre and television from the 1950s to the present day.

In the early days of his film career, before he had made the Bond films, the publicity departments used to list some of his previous occupations: dray-horse driver, sailor (he joined the Navy for a short period at seventeen), labourer, cement mixer, French polisher (of coffins), artist's model (at Edinburgh College of Art), lifeguard, machine-minder and weight lifter. Connery was quoted as saying: 'I've learnt far more about acting from the jobs I've done in the past than any dramatic academy could teach. It's experience from *real* life that's valuable in this profession. And the more jobs you do before becoming an actor the better.'

There was a time, long since past, when Connery was identified with one role, and one role only, and the public at large did not seem interested in seeing him in anything else, exacerbating to an actor who does not wish to be typecast and had already appeared in a wide range of parts, including roles in Euripides, Shakespeare, Synge, O'Neill, Pirandello, Giraudoux, Anouilh, Miller, Rattigan and Tolstoy.

His parts, over the years, have included road haulage driver, welder, boxer, journalist, gypsy, detective, burglar, stoker, poet, farmer, terrorist, explorer, exterminator, airport security chief, NASA scientist, marshal, mercenary, television reporter, cowboy, sheikh, professor (an authority on the Holy Grail), publisher and monk. He has served in the Army, Navy and Air Force and played kings, emperors and warriors, including Alexander the Great, Agamemnon, Richard the Lionheart, Robin Hood, Macbeth and Ahmad ibn Muhammad Raisuli, Sheriff of the Berbers.

In his time he has married a kleptomaniac, murdered his uncle, been murdered by his mother, defected to Russia, defected to America, committed incest in Switzerland, knocked about India with his mate, been hanged in Massachusetts and Pennsylvania, robbed a train in England, robbed an entire apartment block on Fifth Avenue, researched a cure for cancer in the Brazilian jungle, had his head chopped off, and lived for 2437 years. . . .

Sean (né Thomas) Connery was born on 25 August 1930 in Edinburgh. He made his first appearance on stage in 1953 in the Anna Neagle musical, *Sixty Glorious Years,* when it visited Edinburgh and needed tall actors to be guardsmen. Some

time later, having travelled down to London to represent Scotland in a Mr Universe competition, he auditioned for the first national tour of Rodgers and Hammerstein's *South Pacific,* landing a job in the chorus, and stayed with the show for the next year and a half, graduating to a small part, and changing his name to Sean.

By the end of 1955, he was appearing in weekly rep at the Q Theatre in Kew, playing small roles in Agatha Christie's *Witness for the Prosecution,* Jean Anouilh's *Point of Departure* and Dolph Dorman's *A Witch in Time,* before being cast as the maintopman in *The Good Sailor,* an adaptation of Herman Melville's *Billy Budd,* at the Lyric, Hammersmith, early in 1956.

He acted in three plays at the Oxford Playhouse, at the time one of the most adventurous regional theatres. His roles were: Pentheus, the tyrant king, in Euripides' *The Bacchae* (1959); Mat Burke, the Irish stoker, to Jill Bennett's Anna in Eugene O'Neill's *Anna Christie* (1960); and the seducer in Luigi Pirandello's *Naked* (1960), opposite his wife Diane Cilento, with whom he had already acted in *Anna Christie* on television three years earlier. He toured in Jess Gregg's *The Sea Shell* (1959), with Sybil Thorndike, and also acted with her on television in J. M. Synge's one-acter, *Riders to the Sea* (1960), playing her son.

In 1962 Connery appeared on the West End stage for the first and last time as Holofernes in an unsuccessful English premiere of Jean Giraudoux's *Judith.* His only connection with the theatre thereafter has been to co-produce a transfer of the Oxford Playhouse production of Ben Jonson's *Volpone* (starring Leo McKern and Leonard Rossiter) and to direct Cilento in *I've Seen You Cut Lemons* (1969) by Ted Allan Herman, whose previous play, *The Secret of the World,* he had hoped to direct in New York with Shelley Winters. *The Secret of the World* never materialised and *I've Seen You Cut Lemons* opened and closed in the same week.

Connery's career in television began with walk-ons. His big break came in 1957 when Jack Palance, who was to have repeated his American TV success in *Requiem for a Heavyweight* in England, withdrew at the last minute. Alvin Rakoff, the producer, offered him the leading role and his success as the boxer won him a contract with Twentieth Century-Fox.

He played John Proctor in Arthur Miller's *The Crucible* (1959), and Hotspur in *An Age of Kings* (1960), an adaptation of Shakespeare's history cycle. His choleric, chivalrous and vigorous performance was highly praised. In 1960 he also acted with Michael Hordern in Giles Cooper's *Without the Grail,* with Françoise Rosay and Dorothy Tutin in Jean Anouilh's *Colombe,* and with Robert Shaw in *The Pets,* an adaptation of Shaw's novel, *The Hiding Place,* the story of a mad German corporal who kept two members of a crashed British bomber crew as his prisoners in his cellar, long after the War had ended. He played Macbeth on Canadian television, a role he had been offered in the theatre by Joan Littlewood at Stratford East, and turned down.

In 1961 Connery appeared as Alexander the Great in Terence Rattigan's *Adventure Story* and as Vronsky to Claire Bloom's Anna in Leo Tolstoy's *Anna Karenina*. The latter was based on a play rather than the original novel, which resulted in some heavy-handed theatrical confrontations. He cut a handsome, if novelette, figure in uniform, but out of it was too modern. Since then he has been seen in Alun Owen's *MacNeil* (1969), playing a lecherous master carpenter, and made two documentaries, *The Bowler and the Bunnet* (1967), about Clydeside, and *Sean Connery's Edinburgh* (1982), both narrated and directed by himself.

Connery's film career began with small parts in *No Road Back* (a crime story, 1956), *Hell Drivers* (a manic road movie, 1957), *Time Lock* (a gripping little suspense thriller, 1957), and *Action of the Tiger* (an adventure story, 1957).

He acted opposite Lana Turner, as her lover, in *Another Time, Another Place* (1958) and then opposite Gordon Scott, as one of the villains, in *Tarzan's Greatest Adventure* (1959). He was one of the big people in *Darby O'Gill and the Little People* (1959), all Irish whimsy and trick photography, playing the romantic juvenile lead. By 1961, he was starring in *The Frightened City*, a British *film noir*, and in *On the Fiddle*, a wartime farce with Alfred Lynch. He also played a bit part (like everybody else) in the Darryl F. Zanuck all-star D-Day epic, *The Longest Day* (1962).

Dr. No (1962), directed by Terence Young, with whom he had first worked in *Action of the Tiger*, was cheaply made and looked it. After a slow start it became the second most popular movie of the year in the UK, its success taking everybody by surprise, though not Felix Barker, the *Evening News* critic, who predicted it would make a fortune. Arthur Knight, in *Saturday Review*, declared it was 'the best bad film of the year'. Three more Bond films followed at yearly intervals. *From Russia With Love*, directed by Terence Young, was the top money-making British film in the UK in 1963. *Goldfinger*, directed by Guy Hamilton, was equally successful and reached No. 3 in the American charts in 1964. *Thunderball*, directed by Terence Young, was No. 1 in both the UK and the USA in 1965. 007 had become the international cult hero of the '60s and Connery was the biggest international star in the business.

The great strength of his nonchalant and polished performance was that he transformed Ian Fleming's quintessential public-school hero into a rougher

mould and stepped outside of the character in a manner which allowed him to mock Bond and his criminal, carnal and cock-eyed adventures. Preposterously invincible and no less preposterously virile, 007 was a joke, lethally and sexually; and the humour was dry, Martini-dry.

During the above period he made *Woman of Straw* (directed by Basil Dearden, 1964), a macabre baroque thriller in need of a macabre baroque director. He also made *Marnie* (1964) for Alfred Hitchcock, a disturbing psychological melodrama of female frigidity and masculine lust, which ranks amongst Hitchcock's best, though it was not thought so at the time, especially by those who had come hoping for another *Psycho* and *The Birds,* and found the more subtle thrills of *Vertigo.*

Always anxious to escape from Bondage and to do films that would offer him a fresh creative challenge (even though he knew there would be less of a market for such films), Connery made *The Hill* (1965), a savage and loud indictment of army brutality, working with Sidney Lumet for the first time. He then appeared opposite Joanne Woodward as the randy poet in *A Fine Madness* (directed by Irvin Kershner, 1966), a satiric portrait of the artist at war with society. There were many critics who thought (mistakenly) he should stick to Bond. Yet by the time *You Only Live Twice,* directed by Lewis Gilbert, appeared on the screens in 1967, there had been so many imitations of the genre that the same critics (though not the public) felt the series had come to the end of the road.

Edward Dmytryk's *Shalako* (1968), following in the wake of the popular spaghetti Westerns, was described as Britain's first excursion into large-scale Western. It was to be her last. Despite the casting of Connery and Brigitte Bardot, it failed at the box office. As did, sadly, Martin Ritt's *The Molly Maguires* (1969), a much more impressive work, set in the last century, which drew its parallels with the Civil Rights Movement in the 1970s and made a strong statement on unrest and violence. *The Molly Maguires,* the first of Connery's political polemics, was a major film and is long overdue for reappraisal.

He was brought in to play the peripheral role of Roald Amundsen in *La Tenda Rossa (The Red Tent,* directed by Mikhail Kalatozov, 1969), after most of the film had been completed, in an attempt to make the movie more commercial outside of Europe. Its release was delayed by four years in England. In 1971 he enjoyed a commercial hit in Sidney Lumet's expert thriller *The Anderson Tapes,* whose real subject matter was the uses and abuses of electronic surveillance equipment by public and private agencies.

Most of the critics, who had sat through *Casino Royale* (a send-up of a send-up), greeted *Diamonds Are Forever* (directed by Guy Hamilton, 1971) with delight,

Opposite: Sean Connery as James Bond.   11

declaring it was the best Bond film yet. It wasn't, and Connery, who had never made any secret of his dissatisfaction with the limitations of the role, announced he would never play Bond again. He went on to make his first venture into independent film-making with *The Offence* (1972), which was based on Anthony Hopkins's claustrophobic and harrowing play. Directed by Sidney Lumet, he gave one of the finest performances of his career as a detective who beats a suspected child-molester to death during an interrogation.

He worked with John Boorman, in Ireland, on his expressionistic *Zardoz* (1973), a satiric saga, set in the Dark Ages some two hundred years hence, which drew on Jonathan Swift's nightmare vision of the geriatric Struldbrugs, who were condemned to live for ever. *Ransom* (1974), directed by Casper Wrede, best known for his work in the classical theatre, got a really bad press, which was a bit unfair since it was perfectly acceptable as an undemanding low-key thriller.

Sidney Lumet, having persuaded Connery to play a bit part in Agatha Christie's *Murder on the Orient Express* (1974), was then able to persuade thirteen other stars to do the same. The film was immensely popular, and its popularity led to an unending Christie revival on big and small screens alike, the 1930s lovingly and expensively recreated with all-star casts.

Three major roles followed in quick succession, a trio of larger-than-life heroes. The first was Raisuli, the Sheriff of the Berbers, in John Milius's *The Wind and the Lion* (1975), an epic romantic desert adventure, which was also a satire on gunboat diplomacy, with some witty juxtapositions of the barbaric East and so-called civilised West. Then there was Daniel Dravot in Rudyard Kipling's *The Man Who Would Be King* (1975), directed by John Huston, a story of comradeship and greed in the familiar Huston manner. Dravot, absurd yet ultimately tragic in his vaulting ambition and blasphemy, remains one of the best things Connery has done and is, not surprisingly, one of his favourite parts. The third role, another fine performance, was Robin Hood in Richard Lester's *Robin and Marian* (1976), which was not nearly as sentimental as its title suggested; rather was it a bitter-sweet lament on the death of the outlaw, concerned with the mythology of being a hero and exploring what it was like to be middle-aged in the Middle Ages. It was too European a movie to succeed at the American box office.

The Next Man (directed by Richard C. Sarafian, 1976), a complex thriller, in which he played a Saudi Arabian minister, also did very badly in the United States, and received only a limited showing in Britain. He had one of the more substantial roles in Richard Attenborough's all-star *A Bridge Too Far* (1977), the story of the Battle of Arnhem in World War II, and then went on to play the first man to attempt a robbery on a moving train in Michael Crichton's *The First Great*

Train Robbery (1978), an enjoyable period romp, directed and acted with engaging humour and tension.

Ronald Neame's *Meteor* (1979) was not so much a disaster movie as a disaster. Richard Lester's *Cuba* (1979), mixing romance and revolution during the last days of the Batista regime, was better but deeply flawed and is now largely forgotten.

Connery made a guest appearance as Agamemnon in animator Terry Gilliam's *Time Bandits* (1981). He did what a man had to do in Peter Hyams's *Outland* (1981), playing a marshal in a space frontier, and he did what a man didn't have to do in Richard Brooks's *The Man With The Deadly Lens* (1982, known in America as *Wrong Is Right*), playing a television reporter peddling violence as entertainment.

Five Days One Summer (1982), an elegiac miniature in epic surroundings, directed by Fred Zinnemann (of *High Noon* fame, a film Connery much admired), deserves to be much better known, which is more than can be said for Stephen Weeks's *Sword of the Valiant* (1983), a dire version of *Sir Gawain and the Green Knight*.

In 1983, twelve years after Connery had said he would never play Bond again, he returned to his old role in *Never Say Never Again* (the title suggested by his present wife, Micheline), directed by Irvin Kershner. Three years later he was cast as the 2437-years-old Ramirez in Russell Mulcahy's *Highlander*, a violent and romantic saga, aimed at a teenage audience, and acted with the sort of braggadocio he, no doubt, would have brought to Tom Stoppard's *Rosencrantz and Guildenstern Are Dead*, had he not fallen ill and had to withdraw from the production. He also appeared, unwisely, in the sequel, *Highlander II* (1991).

Umberto Eco's *Der Name der Rose* (*The Name of the Rose*, directed by Jean-Jacques Annaud, 1986) was one of the key films of the 1980s and a major turning point in Connery's career, winning him many awards, and which he consolidated when he won further prizes and his first Oscar for his role, as the Irish beat-cop, in Brian de Palma's *The Untouchables* (1987), the most popular gangster movie since *The Godfather*.

Peter Hyams's routine thriller, *The Presidio* (1988), which followed, was a retrograde step, but fortunately only a momentary blip, before Steven Spielberg's enormously successful *Indiana Jones and the Last Crusade* (1989), a wonderfully ridiculous adventure story and, at the same time, a loving recreation of the adventure genre. Its success was due in no small part to the brilliant idea of casting the hero of the 1960s as the father of the hero of the 1980s. Having played Harrison Ford's dad, Connery then went on to play Dustin Hoffman's dad and Matthew Broderick's granddad in *Family Business* (1989), which, in the event,

Opposite: Sean Connery in *Indiana Jones and the Last Crusade.*

wasn't such a good idea.

John McTiernan's *The Hunt for Red October* (1990), a Cold War movie, was out of date by the time it was released; not that it made a scrap of difference to the box-office returns. Having made one political statement, Connery immediately proceeded to make another, cast as the saxophone-playing publisher in the John le Carré romantic thriller, *The Russia House* (1990), a story of three disillusioned people, directed by Fred Schepisi.

He made a last-minute 'surprise' appearance as Richard I in Kevin Costner's *Robin Hood – Prince of Thieves* (1991), though very few people were surprised, it being the least well-kept secret of the year. In 1992 he played a scientist researching a cure for cancer in the Brazilian jungle in *Medicine Man,* directed by John McTiernan.

Sean Connery, a great Scottish patriot, is an actor of powerful physical presence, natural grace and seeming effortless subtlety. Once the definitive permissive hero of the 1960s, he is now the screen's elder statesman, enjoying an Indian summer, more popular and more successful than he has ever been. The pages which follow are a pictorial tribute to the authority, magnetism, sexual charisma, integrity and humour he brings to his acting and also an acknowledgement of the enormous pleasure his performances have given and continue to give to the public, the critics and the acting profession alike.

The 1950s

NO ROAD BACK

directed by Montgomery Tully   1956

Sean Connery and
Paul Carpenter in
No Road Back.

Connery made his film debut in this heavy-handed and improbable thriller cast as a member of a gang of criminals carrying out one last big diamond robbery. The film was notable for its blind and deaf fence (Margaret Rawlings) who was finally locked in a room with a killer. She had a gun in one hand and a guide dog in the other.

Excellent film actors like Alfie Bass, Philip Ray, Sean Connery and Eleanor Summerfield go through the motions of performing in parts that have no lines worth speaking and no distinguishable identities.

Tribune

REQUIEM FOR A HEAVYWEIGHT

directed by Alvin Rakoff   BBC television   1957

Mountain McClintock, who had once been in the running for the world title, was no longer allowed to fight because another fight might well have blinded him. Humiliated and bewildered, he made a dismal circuit of the employment agencies. The role was a major turning point in Connery's career and led to a film contract.

This is neither a fragrant play nor a tribute to the noble art. But its producer, Alvin Rakoff, let it have every chance, and the dramatist ought to go down on his knees to Sean Connery, with or without gore-blood.

The Listener

Although physically miscast as the fighter ('a mouthful of teeth and a voice like General Lee') Mr Sean Connery played with a shambling and articulate charm that almost made his love affair credible.

The Times

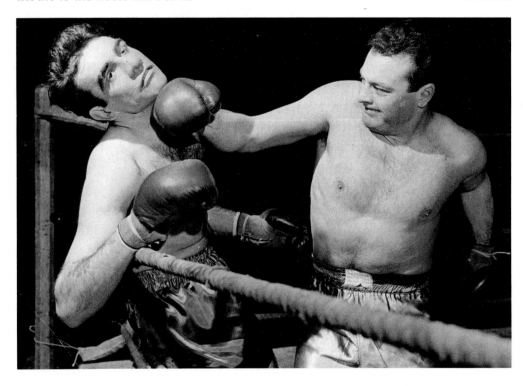

Sean Connery and George Margo in *Requiem for a Heavyweight*.

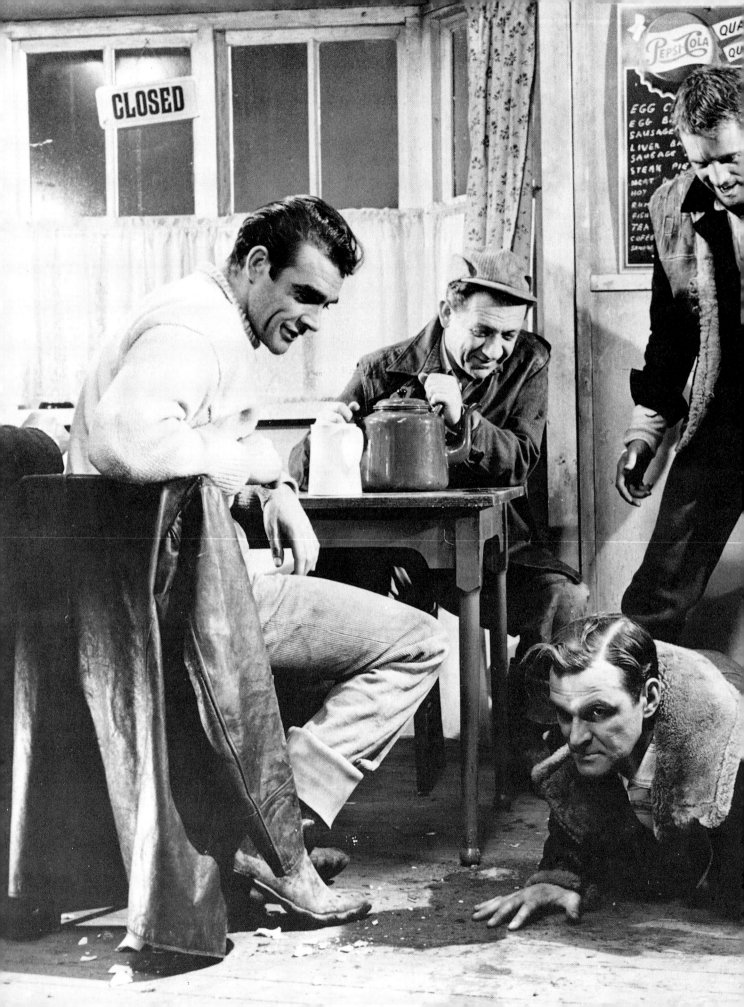

HELL DRIVERS
directed by C. Raker Endfield   1957

Hell Drivers, the British film industry's answer to *On the Waterfront*, was a tough melodrama about the exploitation of road haulage drivers by unscrupulous contractors. The wages were good, but the roads were treacherous, and any driver who fell below the minimum number of hauls (twelve per day) was immediately sacked. The cast was headed by Patrick McGoohan and Stanley Baker. Connery was one of the drivers.

There are some good individual performances, but the film, though produced with efficiency and assurance, is disagreeable and occasionally vicious.

Monthly Film Bulletin

The hell drivers themselves appear like a collection of Bad American actors with impeccable English accents.

Times Educational Supplement

Sean Connery, Sidney James, Stanley Baker and Patrick McGoohan in *Hell Drivers*.

TIME LOCK

directed by Gerald Thomas   1957

John Paul,
Murray Kash
and Sean Connery
in *Time Lock*.

A little boy was accidentally shut in an impregnable vault of a Toronto bank, time-locked to open after sixty-three hours. This modest, small-scale Canadian film was a neat, nerve-racking race against time, with fire brigade, police, bank staff and acetylene welders, all co-operating to break into the vault.

The boy was played by Vincent Winter, the young star of *Kidnappers.* Connery played one of the welders, here seen about to direct flames at a door constructed to resist fire.

ACTION OF THE TIGER

directed by Terence Young   1957

Sean Connery,
Martine Carol and
Van Johnson in
Action of the Tiger.

IT'S RAW! IT'S ROUGH! IT'S ROMANTIC! screamed the poster. *Action of the Tiger* was a rambling *Boys' Own* adventure with Van Johnson and Martine Carol in the leading roles, falling in love and rescuing refugee children in communist Albania.

Connery had the small part of a tough sailor, who propositioned the heroine and got beaten up. The scenery and Herbert Lom, cast as a comic pantomime brigand, got the best notices.

Altogether this is the kind of picture a child cuts from the back of a corn flake packet.

ANTHONY CARTHEW *Daily Herald*

23

ANOTHER TIME, ANOTHER PLACE

directed by Lewis Allen   1958

Lana Turner and
Sean Connery in
*Another Time,
Another Place.*

Another Time, Another Place was a World
War II soap opera. An American journalist (Lana Turner, in mink) falls in
love with a BBC commentator (Sean
Connery), only to discover, a week after
his death in an air crash, that he was
married, and his wife (Glynis Johns) and
her little boy are alive and well in a
Cornish fishing village.

There is, however, something wrong in the love-life of Miss Turner and her beetling-browed, unctuous-voiced BBC man (a newcomer to films, called Sean Connery, who will not, I guess, grow old in the industry).

DEREK MONSEY *Sunday Express*

Connery, in his first big part, gives the impression that he is reading his lines from a none-too-helpful prompt book.

ANTHONY CARTHEW *Daily Herald*

Sean Connery and Glynis Johns in *Another Time, Another Place.*

DARBY O'GILL AND THE LITTLE PEOPLE

directed by Robert Stevenson   1959

A film for those who have never seen a leprechaun.

Darby O'Gill (Albert Sharpe) spent all day in the pub, telling stories about his encounters with the little people and their king (Jimmy O'Dea). The lord of the manor sacked him and gave his job of caretaker to a handsome and charming young Dublin man (Sean Connery), who sang his way into the heart of Darby's daughter (Janet Munro) and chased her across the fields. 'I like a lively girl,' he said. He had a winning and sexy smile. He also beat up the village bully (Keiron Moore), the fight being registered almost entirely in Darby's agonised facial reactions.

Darby O'Gill and the Little People was wholesome Walt Disney family fare; though the arrival of the Banshee, the macabre Death Coach with the headless coachman, scared an awful lot of little children out of their wits. It was reported in the Press, that after one school-showing at a Christmas party, an embarrassed headmistress found herself having to write three hundred notes of apology to parents.

Leprecorn by Walt Disney for leprechauns only.

FRED MAJDALNY *Daily Mail*

Sean Connery and Janet Munro in *Darby O'Gill and the Little People.*

26

THE BACCHAE

a play by Euripides   directed by Minos Volanakis   The Playhouse, Oxford   1959

The Bacchae, the last of the great Greek plays, was written while Euripides was in exile, circa 407 BC. This performance was thought to be the first professional production in England in fifty years.

King Pentheus attempted to stamp out the cult of Dionysos and to deny him his birthright. Dionysos took a terrible revenge. Pentheus was torn to pieces by his mother, Argave, and her female companions at a Bacchanal.

Connery played the tyrant king whose puritanism was seen as a cloak for his latent voyeurism and transvestism. Michael David was Dionysos and Yvonne Mitchell was Argave.

Pentheus is here brilliantly conceived as a prurient Calvinist watch committee man, with a sick desire to spy on nameless orgies. His hubris lies in his attempt to subdue the sensual part of man.

ERIC KEOWN *Manchester Guardian*

Mr Sean Connery gives the heartsick Pentheus exactly the right exasperated bullying impatience until the moment when his unconscious desires betray him.

DAVID MORGAN *New Statesman*

Sean Connery's Pentheus was too much on the surface and his American inflections were often infuriating.

FRANK DIBB *Plays and Players*

Michael David and Sean Connery in *The Bacchae.*

TARZAN'S GREATEST ADVENTURE

directed by John Guillermin   1959

Sean Connery in
*Tarzan's Greatest
Adventure.*

Tarzan made his first appearance on the screen in 1918. Forty years later, Apeman (Gordon Scott) was more civilised, but he was still having to cope with crocodiles, deadly spiders, snakes, man-eating lions, cannibals, treacherous swamps, quick-sands, and a ruthless gang of diamond smugglers, led by Anthony Quayle. Connery was one of the villains. Tarzan shot him with his bow and arrow.

THE CRUCIBLE

directed by Henry Kaplan   BBC television   1959

Sean Connery and
Susannah York in
The Crucible.

The Crucible, one of the great twentieth-century plays, based on the notorious witchcraft trials in Salem, Massachusetts, in 1692, came directly out of Arthur Miller's own experiences of Senator Joe McCarthy's witch-hunt of communists in the 1950s.

Connery played John Proctor, who chose to be hanged rather than incriminate others and sign a document, declaring that he had been trafficking with the Devil.

Mr Sean Connery, powerfully virile as the husband, and Mr Noel Willman, formidably chilly as the savage governor, carried off the acting honours.

The Times

Opposite: Sean Connery as James Bond.

The 1960s

ANNA CHRISTIE

a play by Eugene O'Neill   directed by Douglas Seale   The Playhouse, Oxford   1960

Mat Burke is a powerful, broad-chested six footer, his face handsome in a hard, rough, bold, defiant way. He is about thirty, in the full power of his heavy-muscled, immense strength.

EUGENE O'NEILL

Mat, the bragging Irish stoker, fell in love with Anna Christie, believing her to be the only really decent woman he had ever known. When he learned she had been a prostitute, he was so shattered he wanted to kill her.

O'Neill's ballad-like drama should have ended in murder; instead it ended in marriage, an unlikely climax, intended, no doubt, to satisfy the original 1921 Broadway audience and send them home happy. Jill Bennett played Anna.

Mat Burke was a role Connery had already played on television, opposite Diane Cilento in 1957.

Mr Connery seized happily upon Mat's Irish braggadocio and also illuminated the man's alternating savagery and tenderness with unfailing conviction.

FRANK DIBB *Plays and Players*

Sean Connery's Mat Burke is powerfully compounded of Irish bravado and, in the more sincere moods of the character, an almost strangulated simplicity of utterance.

Stage

Sean Connery is magnificent as Mat Burke.

Oxford Times

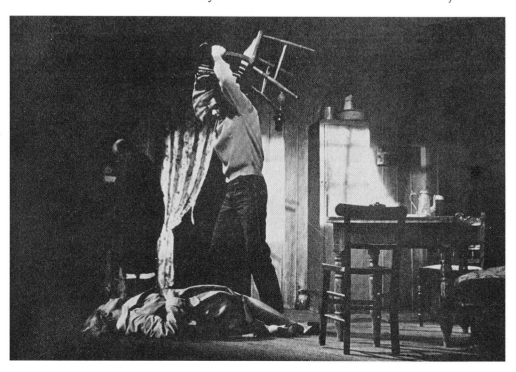

Jill Bennett and Sean Connery in *Anna Christie.*

NAKED

a play by Luigi Pirandello   directed by Minos Volanakis   The Playhouse, Oxford   1960

Sean Connery and Diane Cilento in *Naked*.

Minos Volanakis's production was a rare opportunity to see one of Luigi Pirandello's less well-known plays.

Are we really as we see ourselves? Or are we as others see us? A woman (Diane Cilento) attempted to commit suicide, and failed. Her story was told by a number of people: by the woman herself, giving a highly romantic account of her life to a journalist; by the men in her past (including Sean Connery); and by a seedy Roman novelist, who befriended her and turned her story into his fiction. The play ended with the woman attempting to commit suicide for a second time and succeeding.

As the seducer torn between lust and remorse Mr Sean Connery makes a curiously unforgettable impression.

The Times

Sean Connery, as the seducer who wrecked his life by embarking on a love affair with the girl, carries his burden of guilt nobly and with a finely withdrawn power.

JON HARTRIDGE *Oxford Mail*

THE FRIGHTENED CITY

directed by John Lemont   1961

Opposite:
Herbert Lom and
Sean Connery in
The Frightened City.

Below:
Sean Connery,
Herbert Lom and
Alfred Marks in
The Frightened City.

Chicago came to London. *The Frightened City* was about organised protection and gang warfare in the sleazy West End. The detective-in-charge (John Gregson), lacking manpower and proof, argued that what he needed was more men and a law designed to catch the thieves and not hamper the police. 'I don't want my kids growing up in a world run by scum like that,' he said, referring to Alfred Marks in his role of slimy mobster.

What he wanted was a straight-up-and-down villain, as represented by Sean Connery, cast as the best cat-burglar in the business, lured into the protection racket, and finally persuaded by the detective to testify against the top man, a very smooth operator, played by Herbert Lom.

Dark, rugged and handsome Connery prowled round the ghastly cardboard sets, which were so characteristic of the British movies of the period. He was like a panther. While he was taking a shower in the gymnasium, his girlfriend burst in. 'Are you decent?' she asked. 'Only when I have to be,' he replied. The innuendoes would come in very handy in his future career.

Connery is a rangy, virile young man who combines toughness, charm and Irish blarney.

Variety

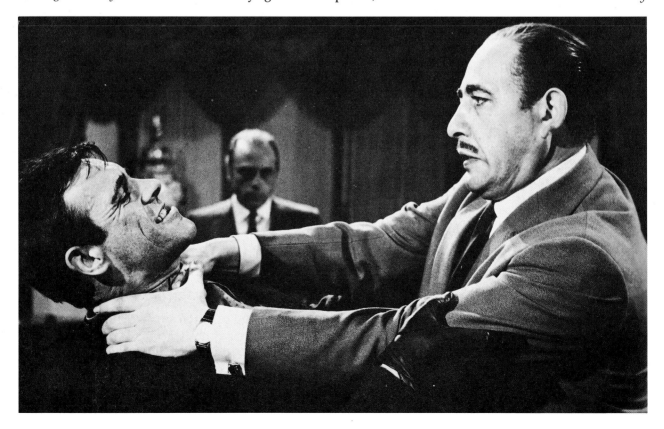

ADVENTURE STORY

directed by Rudolph Cartier   BBC television   1961

Sean Connery in
Adventure Story.

Adventure Story, a portrait of Alexander the Great, was a television adaptation of Terence Rattigan's West End play. Connery played Alexander, a role created in the theatre by Paul Scofield.

Mr Sean Connery, the conqueror in thrall to his own conquests, recognising but unable to resist the corruptions of power, played with intelligence and well directed force; he never, even as a reluctant tyrant, completely lost the impetuous charm on which Mr Rattigan insists at the play's opening. Certain inflections and swift deliberations of gesture at times made me feel that the part had found the young Olivier it needs.

The Times

ON THE FIDDLE

directed by Cyril Frankel   1961   US title: *Operation Snafu*   also: *Operation Warhead*

On the Fiddle was a service farce within the context of a real war and its opportunities for black market. A quick-witted cockney spiv (the likeable Alfred Lynch) and a slow-witted gypsy (the likeable Sean Connery) teamed up in the RAF. Never have so few fiddled so many.

The film, poorly scripted, was a string of loosely connected episodes round their exploits. The war-dodgers ended up as war heroes, in a silly and inappropriate coda, which saw them in reluctant action in the Ardennes. Their roles were suddenly reversed, the gypsy proving much the braver and more resourceful of the two.

Connery, brawny yet gentle as a babe, was a nice bloke, his conscience, his heart, and everything else, in the right place, especially when he arrived to seduce his superior officer (Eleanor Summerfield) with a bunch of lilacs in his mouth.

The supporting cast included practically every comedy actor in the business: Cecil Parker, Wilfrid Hyde White, Stanley Holloway, Kathleen Harrison, Patsy Rowlands, John Le Mesurier, Bill Owen and Ian Whittaker among them. The majority were sadly under-used.

Alfred Lynch and Sean Connery in *On the Fiddle.*

JUDITH

a play by Jean Giraudoux   translated by Christopher Fry
directed by Harold Clurman   Her Majesty's Theatre   1962

H.M. Tennents, the West End management, clearly hoping to repeat the big success they had had with Jean Giraudoux's *Tiger at the Gates (La Guerre de Troie N'Aura Pas Lieu)*, employed the same translator and the same director, but the twenty-three-year-old play was a bore, the production a disaster, the sets and costumes hideous, and the acting poor.

Giraudoux took the familiar biblical story of the Jewish woman, who offered herself to the conqueror to save her people, and fashioned it to his own ornate and pseudo-profound ends. The twist was that Holofernes, God's enemy, behaved nobly and well, while God himself behaved abominably.

'I hope it will be pleasant,' said Judith, a twenty-year-old virgin, as she went into Holofernes's tent, 'something between a crucifixion and uncontrollable laughter.' The night proved even better than she had expected and she killed Holofernes only out of love. The Jews were horrified and the former virgin had to be persuaded (for posterity's sake) that she had killed him out of hatred.

There were moments when it was possible to recognise Giraudoux's hand, notably in those lines in which Holofernes explained why he was a man of the world, but on the whole the writing was so bad it was difficult to see what had attracted Christopher Fry to translate it.

Connery, in an arresting costume, had visible muscular authority as Holofernes.

Sean Connery and Ruth Myers in *Judith*.

Holofernes, as played by Sean Connery, in a gold bikini, suggested an Irish wrestler at the Metropolitan: flights of fancy as when he urges Judith to be a cheerful pagan girl, sat very wryly on him.

PHILIP HOPE-WALLACE
Manchester Guardian

Holofernes played by Mr Sean Connery with a stolid narcissism rather too crude for the vision of pagan freedom against which Jehovah's discipline loses its power.

The Times

There is an operatic performance by Sean Connery as Holofernes.

ROBERT MULLER *Daily Mail*

Ruth Myers and
Sean Connery in
Judith.

THE LONGEST DAY

directed by Darryl F. Zanuck, Andrew Marton, Ken Annakin, Bernhard Wicki   1962

Three million men were keyed up and itching to go. The weather conditions were far from the minimum requirements; but postponement was too bitter to contemplate. 'I don't see that we can possibly do anything but go,' said Eisenhower. The invasion of Europe began on 6 June 1944. Hitler was sound asleep. And nobody dared wake him.

The Longest Day was the most expensive black-and-white epic in the history of the motion picture industry. The film was at its best in its straightforward and quasi-documentary approach rather than in its attempt to inject some personal anecdotes. The set pieces – the strafed beaches, the scaling of the 100-foot cliff-face at Pointe du Hoc under fire, the helicopter shot of an army advancing through a town (in one long shot by Guy Tabary) – were brilliantly organised and photographed.

Perhaps the most memorable sequence, certainly the most moving, was the slaughter of the paratroopers at Sainte-Mère-Eglise. Their parachutes entangled in buildings and trees, the men just hung there, waiting to be picked off one by one, the horror dramatically increased by the sound of the church bell ringing out all the while.

The English actors spoke English, the French actors spoke French, the German actors spoke German, and the American actors spoke American. There were some forty-six stars in cameo roles, including Robert Mitchum, Henry Fonda, Robert Ryan, Robert Wagner, Sal Mineo, Richard Burton, Richard Todd, Jean-Louis Barrault, Madeleine Renaud, Arletty, Curt Jurgens, most of them doing little more than lending their names and familiar faces. Kenneth More, in a characteristically breezy performance, made an instant impact.

Connery turned up very briefly on the Normandy beaches, his zonking smile and eyebrows unmistakable under his helmet.

Opposite:
Norman Rossington
and Sean Connery
in *The Longest Day.*

DR. NO

directed by Terence Young   1962

It was a bit of a joke around town that I was chosen for Bond. The character is not really me at all.

SEAN CONNERY quoted by GEORGE FEIFER
Sunday Telegraph Magazine

Dr. No was described by the Vatican as a dangerous mixture of violence, vulgarity, sadism and sex, which was excellent for business. The film began as the series meant to go on: arch villains, exotic settings, amusing murders, enormous sets, explosive climaxes, beautiful girls who couldn't act, plus a catchy theme tune and bright credit titles, with flashing coloured circles, which made the audience feel as if they were in for a musical.

The first shot of Bond was at the gaming tables, only his fingers and the cards visible, followed by a close-up of his face as he lit a cigarette. The soundtrack played his signature tune. It could have been a commercial for machismo.

Agent 007, licensed to kill, but not to be killed, fought all villains single-handed, surviving water, bullets, fire, electricity. He was a comic-strip hero, a Superman, a Captain Marvel, an immensely good-looking and immensely well-groomed 1930s hero updated to the 1960s. He was cool, sharp and cunning.

Thoroughly professional at all times, fast on the draw, nifty on his feet, nifty in bed, Bond always had time for sex, even if he was already late for his aeroplane and/or about to be murdered. He was the sort of chap who made love to a woman just before he handed her over to the police.

Ian Fleming's hero was an upper-crust

Ursula Andress and Sean Connery in *Dr. No.*

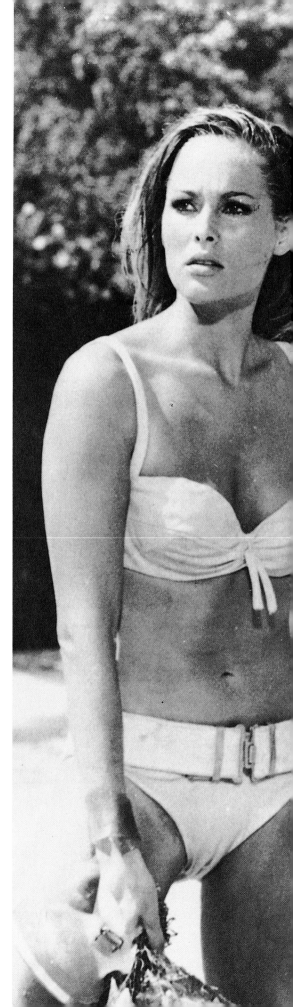

Sean Connery
in *Dr. No.*

cad and a brutal snob. Connery very sensibly sent him up. 'Sergeant, make sure he doesn't get away,' he said, referring to a dead body slumped in the back of his car. Connery was always good with the ironic inflection. 'I think they were on their way to a funeral,' he observed of a hearse which, in its efforts to drive him off the road, had ended up crashing down the mountain side.

Dr. No (Joseph Wiseman in a role turned down by Noël Coward) was a Chinese megalomaniac with no hands. He boasted he was a member of SPECTRE, and a special executive for counter-intelligence. Terrorism, revenge and extortion were his business. He worked from a SF underwater base in the Caribbean, seeking to divert rockets from Cape Canaveral. He was finally boiled to death in his own nuclear reactor.

Radioactive bodies are as good a reason

as any for actors to have to take off their clothes. Ursula Andress, as Honey, archetypical Bond girl, made her entrance from the sea, wearing only a bikini and sheath-knife. (In the novel she entered nude.) 'Did you ever see a mongoose dance?' she asked. 'Or a scorpion with sunstroke sting itself to death? Or a praying mantis eat her husband after making love? I did.' It was probably the last question (far more frightening than the tarantula who made a brief and surprisingly ineffective appearance in Bond's bed) which made 007 delay making love to Honey for so long.

The film had one then bang-up-to-date joke, which was much appreciated at the time, when it was revealed that it was Dr. No who had stolen Goya's portrait of the Duke of Wellington.

Jack Lord and Sean Connery in *Dr. No.*

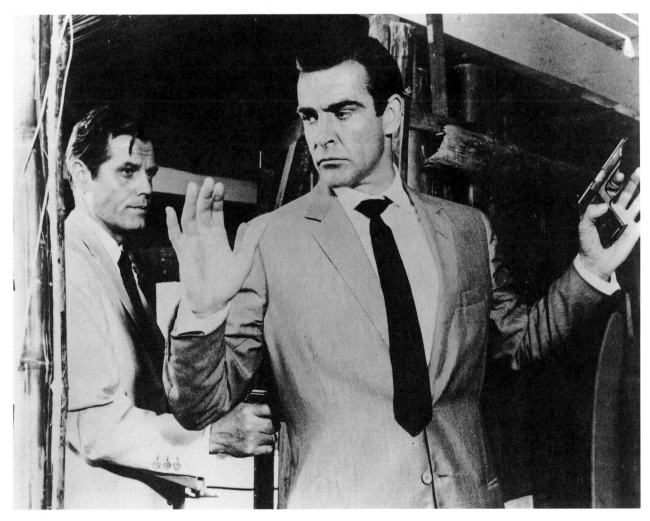

At last Mr Ian Fleming's James Bond makes his bow on the screen, and it is doubtful whether either his admirers or his detractors will recognise him.

The Times

By putting their tongues often enough in their cheeks, the producers manage to turn Ian Fleming's often unsavoury plot ingredients into what you would call sadism for the family.

ALEXANDER WALKER *Evening Standard*

Sean Connery, with his leathery face, Tarzan torso, dark brown Irish voice and arrogant disregard for the deadliest dangers, bestrides a world midway between pre-war Bulldog Drummond and post-war science extravaganza.

CECIL WILSON *Daily Mail*

He looks pretty good. As portrayed by Scotland's Sean Connery, he moves with tensile grace that excitingly suggests the violence that is bottled in Bond.

Time Magazine

Morally the film is indefensible with its lovingly detailed excesses, the contemporary equivalent of watching Christians being fed to lions, and yet its lascivious dedication to violence is a genuine hypnotic . . . The perfect film for a sado-masochistic society.

RICHARD WHITEHALL *Films and Filming*

Left: Sean Connery and Ursula Andress in *Dr. No.*

Right: Joseph Wiseman and Sean Connery in *Dr. No.*

FROM RUSSIA WITH LOVE

directed by Terence Young   1963

James, behave yourself, you are being filmed.

TATIANA ROMANOVA

From Russia With Love, set mainly in Istanbul (with a few tourist shots of Venice thrown in for good measure), was a classier and more expensive movie than *Dr. No.*

The film began with a pre-credit sequence in which Bond was seemingly

Sean Connery in *From Russia With Love.*

Opposite:
Sean Connery and Daniela Bianchi in *From Russia With Love.*

murdered in a moonlit formal garden full of box-tree hedges and classical statues. It then went on to the credits themselves, which were superimposed over the undulating flesh of a belly dancer. There was nothing as good ever again.

The script was surprisingly short of wit until Bond shot an agent making his escape through a window. The house itself was hidden behind an enormous hoarding, advertising *Call Me Bwana,* a film starring Bob Hope and Anita Ekberg. The window was in Ekberg's mouth. 'She should have kept her mouth shut,' he said.

Planes were blown out of the sky, motor-boat chases ended in flames, suitcases exploded on trains, gypsy girls fought over a man (totally irrelevant to the plot), and Bond was chased by a helicopter, the latter a straight crib from Alfred Hitchcock's *North by Northwest*; but the scene with the potential for some original excitement was the chess tournament. The extraordinary thing was, that having gone to the enormous expense of setting the scene up in a glittering *palazzo,* the potential was not even explored, let alone developed.

Bond, gun in one hand and towel round his midriff, met the beautiful and sleepy Tatiana Romanova (Daniela Bianchi) for the first time in bed. The villains included: Lotte Lenya as a lesbian colonel, disguised as a housemaid with a flick knife in her shoe; Robert Shaw as the stoniest of stoney-faced stranglers with a blond crew-cut; Vladek Sheybal as a master chess player; and an unnamed actor, heard but not seen, as their boss, feeding the white pussy on his lap from

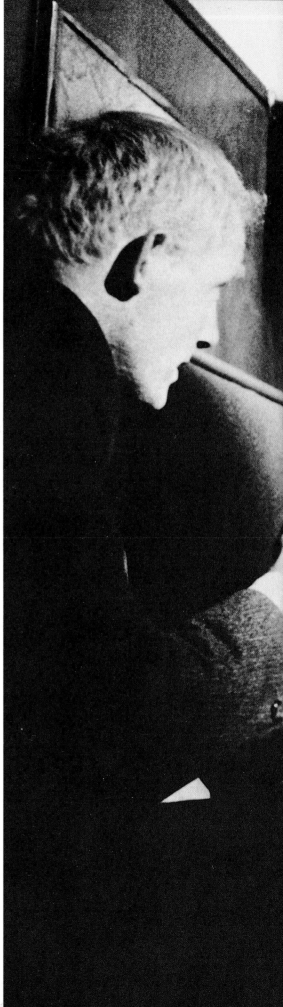

a tank of battling fish.

Connery, immaculate, virile, laconic, kept a straight face and his tongue firmly in cheek throughout.

James Bond is still played by Sean Connery, who has a deal more charm than Fleming's determinedly U-style tough, and who adds considerably to the send-up by being so endearingly non-U in person, bearing an Ulster accent.

DAVID ROBINSON *The Financial Times*

The Bond films are brilliantly skilful. Among other things, they seem to have cottoned on to a kind of brutal flippancy that is the voice of the age.

PENELOPE GILLIAT *The Observer*

Incredible twaddle, it *may* be, but I for one find such twaddle irresistible.

CECIL WILSON *Daily Mail*

What sort of people are we becoming if we can accept such perversions as a giggle?

NINA HIBBIN *Daily Worker*

If Odeon cinemas really think the new Bond film is nice clean fun for all the family, then Britain has some pretty kinky families . . . or soon will have.

Films and Filming

Robert Shaw and Sean Connery in *From Russia With Love.*

It is neither uplifting, instructive, nor life-enhancing. Neither is it great film-making. But it sure is fun.

RICHARD ROUD *Guardian*

WOMAN OF STRAW

directed by Basil Dearden   1964

Sean Connery,
Ralph Richardson,
Gina Lollobrigida
and Laurence Hardy
in *Woman of Straw.*

Woman of Straw, ploddingly directed, was an absurd, glossy old-fashioned murder story, played out in palatial sets by Ken Adams, and acted by Ralph Richardson with good old-fashioned melodramatic relish. He was cast as a crippled millionaire, a sadistic and racist tycoon in a wheelchair, given to humiliating his black servants and being generally obnoxious to everybody. Sir Ralph went on acting even after he had been murdered.

Connery was cast as his sinister nephew, scheming to get his money, evidently the largest fortune in the world. Gina Lollobrigida played the nurse he employed and then persuaded to marry his uncle, hoping to get the cash through her. She was the woman of straw, though you would hardly have thought so from her enormous wardrobe. She spent much of her time getting out of her clothes. Neither actor was convincing.

Gina Lollobrigida
and Sean Connery
in *Woman of Straw*.

Easily the best sequence was the one where the nephew and the nurse were bringing the dead body ashore in the wheelchair and pretending the old man was still alive. However, once the police arrived on the scene, the script fell apart completely, and Connery, who should have been good, was visibly ill at ease, the camera registering far too many blank looks.

The soundtrack used the music of Beethoven, Berlioz, Mozart and Rimsky-Korsakov in a very vulgar way.

In its hammy, ludicrous way it is a reasonably skilful game of hunt-the-murder, but if this is the best Mr Connery can do when he is not playing 007 the sooner he gets back to Bondage the better.

CECIL WILSON *Daily Mail*

Connery, wooden as an old oak beam, looks as if he were desperately wishing he were somewhere else.

ANN PACEY *Daily Herald*

MARNIE

directed by Alfred Hitchcock   1964

Marnie: You don't love me. I'm just something you've caught. You think I'm some kind of animal, you've trapped.

Mark: That's right, you are. I've caught something really wild this time, haven't I? I've caught you, trapped you, and, by God, I'm going to keep you.

Marnie was one of Alfred Hitchcock's psychological thrillers in which the murder came right at the end of the film and was the explanation for all that had gone before.

Marnie ('Tippi' Hedren) was a kleptomaniac. A wealthy publisher, Mark Rutland (Sean Connery), employed her, knowing she was a thief and when he caught her, he offered her a choice – either marriage or prison – only to find on their honeymoon that she could not bear to be handled by men. He accused her of being ill. She retorted that he must be pretty sick himself to be excited by the idea of going to bed with a compulsive thief and pathological liar. The question the honeymoon raised, in some minds, was whether he would rape her before she murdered him. He raped her.

'Tippi' Hedren (in a role originally offered to Princess Grace Kelly of Monaco) was a typical Hitchcock heroine, outwardly glacially cool, well-groomed and blonde. Connery was there to exert a powerful, callous masculine presence and also to act as part-time therapist and zoologist *manqué*, given to reading such works as *The Instinctive Behaviour of the Female Criminal Class* and *Sexual Aberrations of the Female*, the titles themselves

'Tippi' Hedren and Sean Connery in *Marnie*.

54

'Tippi' Hedren, Sean Connery, Louise Lorimer, Martin Gabel and Diane Baker in *Marnie*.

providing the female members of the audience with a good laugh. He brought to his role of predator and sexual blackmailer the ambiguity Cary Grant had brought to his role in *Suspicion*, suggesting that he was as deranged as the heroine and constantly fighting off a powerful impulse to beat the hell out of her.

Mark Rutland boasted that he had trained a tiger to trust him, in much the same way that Petruchio boasted he had trained a hawk to do his bidding. Connery's sexual arrogance, his ironic reactions, incisive questioning and cold-blooded skirmishes, made one wish he had acted not only in *The Taming of the Shrew* but also in Restoration comedy (e.g. Horner in Wycherley's *The Country Wife*) and in Oscar Wilde (e.g. the villain Lord Darlington in *Lady Windermere's Fan* and the hero Lord Goring in *An Ideal Husband*). The performance, like the film, was badly underrated by most critics. Even Hitchcock, in his published conversations with François Truffaut, said he would have preferred to have cast the role

'with a real gentleman, a more elegant man'.

There were three first-class perform-ances in support: from Louise Latham, affecting as Marnie's mother, a wartime prostitute; from Martin Gabel, subtly amusing, as one of Marnie's victims, a lecher who couldn't have cared less about the stolen money but was outraged at the sexual opportunity denied; and from Diane Baker, lemon-pert as a jealous girl who wanted Mark Rutland for herself.

There was a classic Hitchcock sequence in an empty office building at night, where the screen was split down the middle, with a cleaner swabbing in the corridor and the thief opening the safe in the boss's room, both actions visible at the same time, the audience knowing the two people must finally meet. The suspense was enormous.

Sean Connery uses his eyebrows to sardonic effect, but the metallic, private eye voice suggests none of the authority springing from a financially secure upper-crust background.

PETER JOHN DYER *Sight and Sound*

As the patient husband, Connery performs with pallid competence, uncertain whether his role requires him to be a compulsive armchair analyst or a sadist in love.

Time Magazine

As one of Marnie's more willing victims, Sean Connery is served up with an incoherent character (at times his behaviour is even madder than Marnie's) but manages to make it hang together, no mean feat in the circumstances.

RICHARD WHITEHALL *Films and Filming*

Connery, oddly, looks a bit more colourless than he has done with lesser directors.

DAVID ROBINSON *The Financial Times*

Alfred Hitchcock directs Sean Connery in *Marnie*.

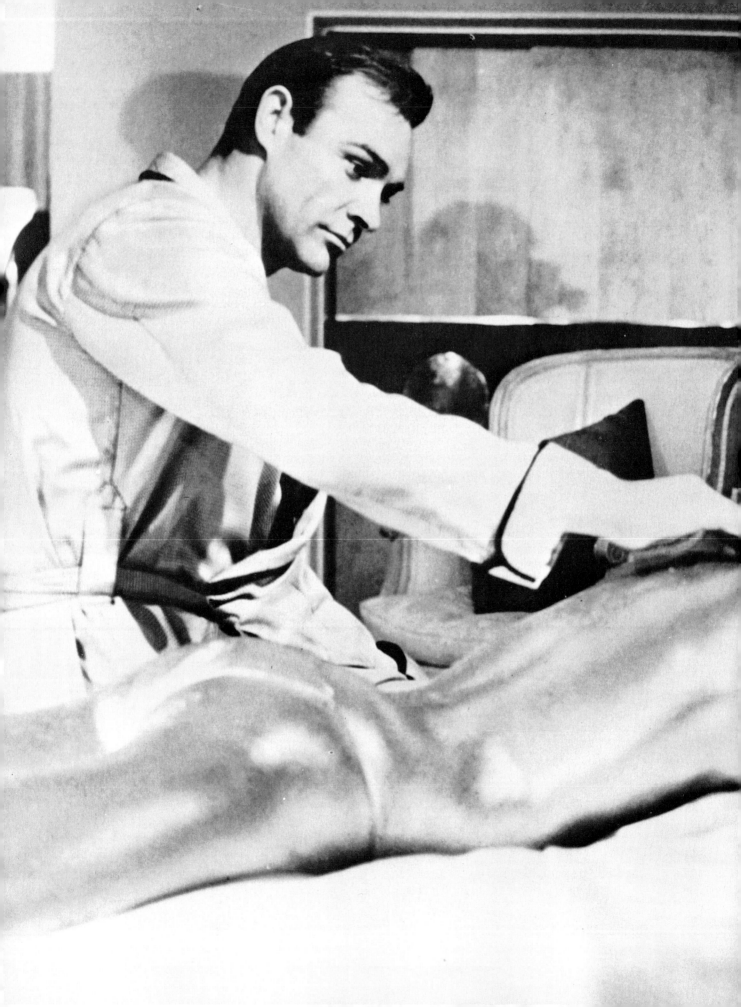

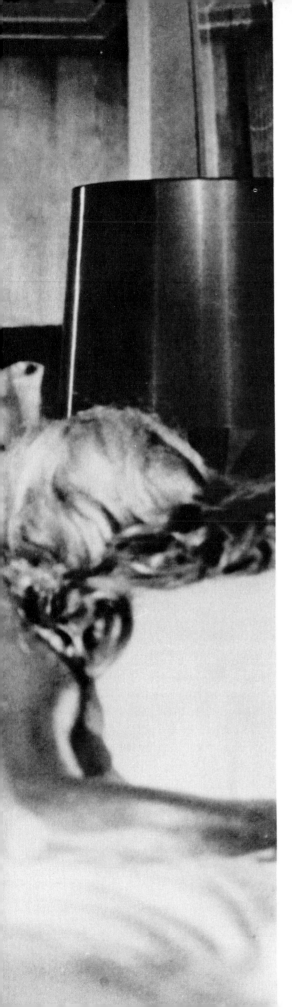

GOLDFINGER

directed by Guy Hamilton   1964

Our violence is carefully plotted. We don't do it promiscuously, we do it tongue-in-cheek. We scale things down a lot because of the visual impact. You may have noticed we avoid using the big screen. All the time we work along with the censor's office.

CUBBY BROCCOLI, Producer, quoted by
JULIAN HOLLAND *Daily Mail*

Goldfinger got off to a big bang, when Bond emerged from the water, in a frog-man suit and with a stuffed seagull on his head, to dynamite a building. Having done the job, he took off his diving suit to reveal that he was wearing an immaculate white dinner jacket underneath. (Cue for the audience to applaud.) 'I have some unfinished business to attend to,' he said, popping off to his girlfriend's bathroom. It was while he was kissing her that he noticed his assailant, reflected in her eye. Ever the gentleman, he quickly turned her round and used her as a battering ram. The assailant ended up in the bath, electrocuted by an electric fire thrown into the water. Only then did the credit titles begin with Shirley Bassey singing the title song. The pace thereafter rarely slackened.

Goldfinger was easily the best Bond film to date, infinitely more professional than *Dr. No* and far superior to *From Russia With Love*. The action was more gripping, the pace faster, the chases more excitingly edited, and the script was wittier, too.

The film was also visually more dramatic and had three memorable images: firstly, a grisly shot of a murdered Shirley Eaton, coated in heavy gold paint;

Sean Connery and Shirley Eaton in *Goldfinger.*

59

secondly, Connery himself spread-eagled on a metal bench, a laser beam cutting between his legs, advancing slowly on his private parts; thirdly, and best of all, a car being crushed in a junkyard, compressed to the size of a tiny cube of steel. It was the knowledge that there was a dead body inside the car which made this sequence so chillingly effective.

The villains were portly and smiling. Gert Frobe played the avuncular Auric Goldfinger, determined to enter Fort Knox and make the United States' gold reserves radioactive for the next fifty-eight years so that he could manipulate the market. Harold Sakata was even more menacing and sinister as his Korean man-servant, who had a lethal bowler. There was also – a characteristic Hitchcock touch this – a dear, sweet, little old lady, who suddenly produced a machine gun and turned Nazi storm-trooper.

Honor Blackman, out of *The Avengers*, was cast as Pussy Galore, a woman of many parts, part villainess, part pilot, part judoist, part lesbian. 'You can turn off the charm,' she told Bond. 'I'm immune.' After a rough-and-tumble in the hay, anticipating the courtship in Franco Zeffirelli's 1976 film of *The Taming of the Shrew* (starring Richard Burton and Elizabeth Taylor), she inevitably found she was not as immune as she had thought, and changed sides.

Not least of the schoolboy pleasures were the technical ingenuity of Ken Adams's designs for Goldfinger's war-room and the interior of Fort Knox. The bullet-proof Aston Martin was also much admired, its modifications including radar, machine-gun headlamps, tyre-slashing knives, smoke screens, flame-throwers, oil slicks and ejector seat. A scaled-down model was presented to the Queen as a present for the young Prince Andrew.

Opposite:
Gert Frobe and
Sean Connery in
Goldfinger.

Below:
Sean Connery in
Goldfinger.

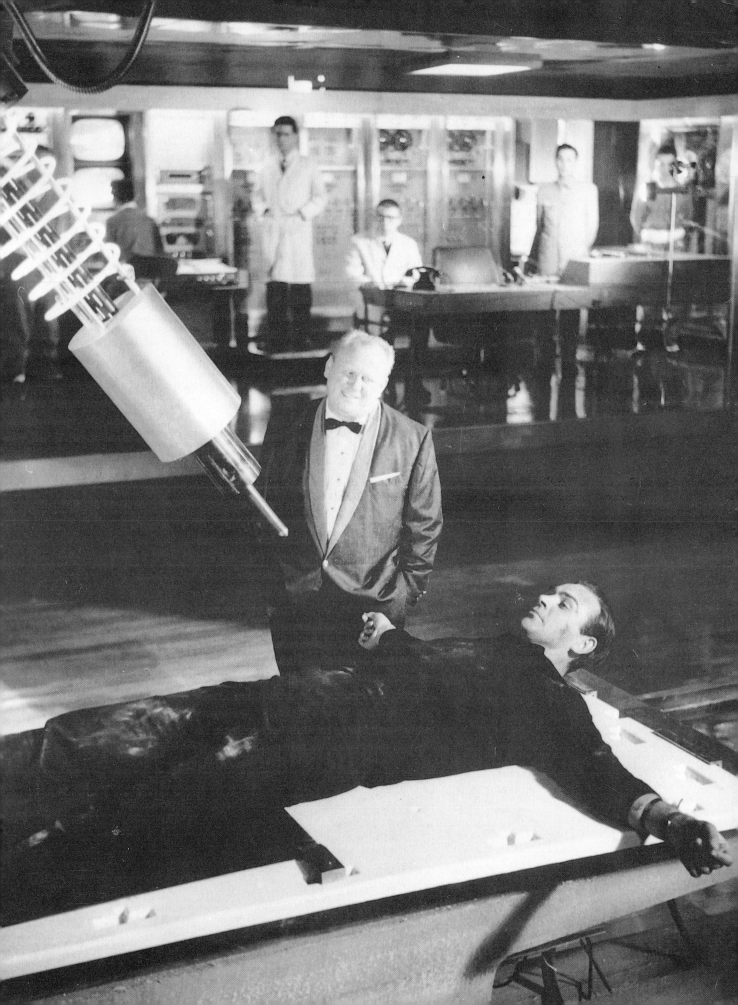

Sean Connery and Honor Blackman in *Goldfinger.*

Who else could play the part now?

ANN PACEY *Sun*

But the real trick of the formula — not, incidentally Ian Fleming's formula at all, but the film's invention — is the way it uses humour. In all his adventures, sexual and lethal, Bond is a kind of joke superman, as preposterously resilient as one of those cartoon cats. . . . *Goldfinger* really is a dazzling object lesson in the principle that nothing succeeds like excess.

Monthly Film Bulletin

There is violence a-plenty but the fantasy is so well created that it doesn't sear the mind; it manages to become quite stimulatingly cathartic.

DEREK PROWSE *The Sunday Times*

When Bond can do *anything* he loses his point: the film becomes a costly *tour de force,* a gigantic firework, expensive purposelessness.

IAN WRIGHT *Guardian*

THE HILL

directed by Sidney Lumet   1965

The subject is the nature of fear; the use of fear as a source of power; and the overcoming of fear as a source of strength.

SIDNEY LUMET

The setting was a military detention camp in the North African desert during World War II. The hill, a man-made pyramid, thirty-five feet high, rising at a sixty-degree angle, was an instrument of torture, run by a brutal RSM (Harry Andrews) and his sadistic staff sergeant (Ian Hendry), who were convinced that the only way to 'make soldiers out of muck' was to break them first. The prisoners were made to double up and down the hill, in the blazing sun, carrying a full army pack until they dropped.

The story focused on five prisoners,

Sean Connery in
The Hill.

63

played by Sean Connery, Alfred Lynch (pathetic misfit), Roy Kinnear (smarmy fat thief), Ossie Davis (West Indian) and Jack Watson (old soldier). Davis provided light relief with some highly popular, if highly unlikely, one-man mutiny in his underpants.

Connery was cast as the only man not to crack, a tough, rugged, steely-eyed warrant-officer, who had been court-martialled for striking an officer and for alleged cowardice under fire, when he had put his conscience above King's Regulations. After the Alfred Lynch character died of exhaustion, he determined to bring the staff sergeant to court martial on a charge of murder.

The film, psychologically overwrought, was a powerful indictment of the abuse of authority and military justice. Some Brits felt deeply offended that it had been entered at the Cannes Film Festival (where it won joint prize for best screenplay).

The Hill, notable for its excellent ensemble work and award-winning black-and-white photography by Oswald Morris, was directed with characteristic rhetorical vigour by Sidney Lumet, building to a bawling climax, which ended with the murder of the staff sergeant. There were fine performances by Michael Redgrave as the weak and ineffectual medical officer, and Ian Bannen, as the only decent, humane screw, who was also gay. The homosexuality, of so many of the characters, was one of the production's less emphatic statements.

The leading role was, undoubtedly, the RSM, a role Connery might have been

Harry Andrews and Sean Connery in *The Hill*.

65

Harry Andrews and
Sean Connery in
The Hill.

expected to play. Harry Andrews was terribly convincing, and in the final scene, dominated more and more by his staff sergeant, his command gradually slipping away from him, he was un-expectedly a tragic figure and very moving.

It needed an actor of Connery's physical and moral stature to stand up to him. The performance was impressive in its economy, and formidable in its display of silent authority. The last image of the film was his anguished face in close-up, roaring at the sheer stupidity of the men taking their personal revenge rather than waiting for the court martial to do it for them.

He gives one of the most disturbingly effective performances of the year . . . It is a masterful portrayal of a caged and anguished animal.

LEONARD MOSLEY *Daily Express*

Rough as thistle, sporting a mustache, he lends muscle presence to a conventional he-man role, and stirs up a hint or two that what has heretofore been sealed in Bond may be the screen's new Gable.

Time Magazine

And there is Sean Connery, with dark, sensitive eyes gazing steadily from his strong face, reminding us what a really splendid actor he is when he is allowed to escape from his stereotyped James Bond image.

MICHAEL THORNTON *Sunday Express*

Sean Connery whose Bond, let's face it, is more suitable for a Silvikrin advert than for the Ian Fleming world, redeems himself by an unassuming, solid performance which is all the stronger in that he never ceases to be only one of a cell-ful of squaddies.

RAYMOND DURGNAT *Films and Filming*

THUNDERBALL

directed by Terence Young   1965

The movie caters to the sexual fantasies of all the married men and half the bachelors of the world.

SEAN CONNERY quoted by *Newsweek*

Much of the action took place in bedrooms, bathrooms, beaches, swimming-pools and health clinics, so that there was maximum opportunity for Bond to take off his clothes and appear in his trunks and towel and show off his hairy chest.

There were beautiful women, any number of killings, a chase through the Mardi Gras, and spectacular car and yacht crashes, before the film reached its underwater climax, an eerie fight between frogmen, dressed in red and black, so that the audience could distinguish the goodies from the baddies, but since

Molly Peters and Sean Connery in *Thunderball*.

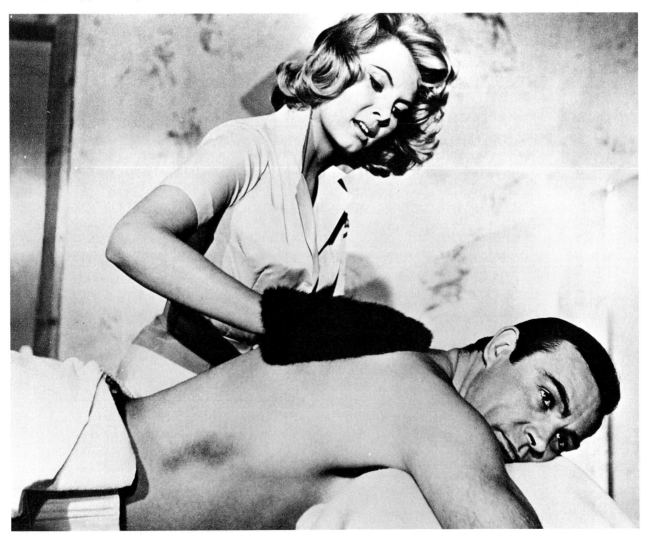

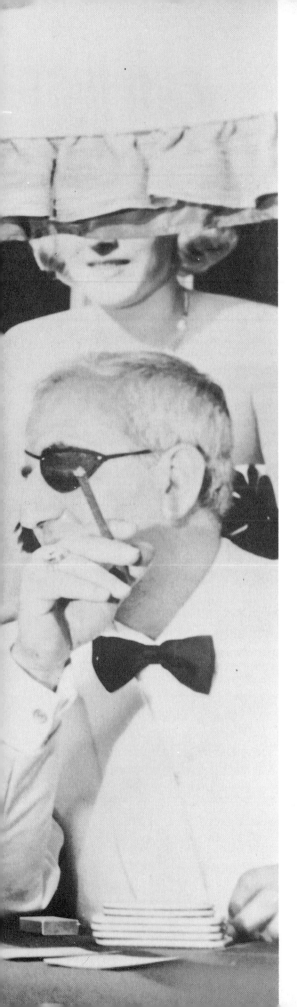

none of them had been seen before, the fact that they were being knifed, harpooned and having their oxygen supply cut, meant little.

Thunderball opened with a funeral. Bond offered the widow, dressed all in black, his sincere condolences with a massive sock to the jaw. The widow was an agent in drag. Bond killed him, pausing only to lift some flowers from a vase and scatter them over the dead body, before making a quick departure by a strap-on rocket.

Bond was as virile as ever. Having just been stretched on an exercise machine, momentarily converted into a medieval torture-rack, he could still make love immediately afterwards with the therapist (Molly Peters) who had rescued him.

Never one to waste time, Bond claimed, with characteristic insolent irony, that he slept only for King and Country. 'You don't think it gave me any pleasure, do you?' As usual he was always quick to use women as a shield, especially if he was going to be shot on a dance-floor. 'Do you mind if my friend sits this one out?' he asked, parking her dead body on a chair.

Nor was he above copulating below water in full skin-diving gear, snorkel, breathing apparatus, flippers, etc. 'I hope we didn't frighten the fish,' he remarked, in the movie's best line, paying compliment to Mrs Patrick Campbell's famous aphorism that she didn't mind what people did, so long as they didn't frighten the horses.

Apart from a dull villain, who wore an eye-patch, and some boringly tame sharks, the real weakness of *Thunderball*

Sean Connery, Claudine Auger and Adolfo Celi in *Thunderball.*

69

Above:
Sean Connery
in *Thunderball*.

Opposite:
Luciana Paluzzi and
Sean Connery in
Thunderball.

was that the gadgets had taken over completely, and Bond (who was off the screen for far too much of the time) had been turned into a comic-strip hero, ridiculously invulnerable, capable of fighting three men at the same time, while steering a boat round dangerous rocks.

The cinema was a duller place before Bond.

DILYS POWELL *The Sunday Times*

But in the raw, racy action of the tale, Connery is better than ever – a maturer, more self-assured hero who wears the role like a glove. A mink one.

DONALD ZEC *Daily Mirror*

It is not just that Sean Connery looks a lot more haggard and less heroic than he did two or three years ago (success can age a man so); but there is much less effort to establish him as the connoisseur playboy. Apart from the off-handed order for Beluga, there is little of that comic display of bon viveur-manship that was one of the charms of Connery's almost-a-gentleman 007.

DAVID ROBINSON *The Financial Times*

But unless things pick up somewhat it will take more than a one-man jet equipment to extract Bond with equal popular success from his next assignment.

The Times

A FINE MADNESS

directed by Irvin Kershner   1966

A Fine Madness was a crazy and relentlessly raucous comedy. Connery was cast as Samson Shillitoe, a frustrated Greenwich Village poet, a fugitive from alimony collectors, lashing out at everybody, leaving a trail of broken furniture, crockery and glass in his wake. Joanne Woodward played his long-suffering waitress-wife, liable to be thrown down the stairs and be socked on the jaw at any moment.

Samson was a compulsive womaniser. Early on there was an amusing office seduction scene when he forgot to turn off a carpet-cleaning machine and there was foam everywhere, the bubbling-over machine providing a graphic visual complement to his unseen actions on the sofa. The highlight of the film, however, was his tipsy lecture to a women's cultural group, a formidable sisterhood of self-satisfied, rich matrons, led by the wonderful Kay Melford, a mountain of flesh. 'Women, have you loved?' he asked them. 'Blossom. Unfold. Open your corsets and bloom. Let the metaphors creep above your knees . . .' The outraged women's fury knew no bounds when he then went on to dismiss them as 'tubercular intestined hags' and the meeting terminated in a riot.

The poet ended up in the clutches of a slick and fashionable New York shrink (Patrick O'Neal), given to wondering what Beethoven, Edgar Allan Poe and Van Gogh might not have achieved had they been in his care. The psychiatrist was quick to agree to a lobotomy after he discovered Samson making love to his wife (Jean Seberg) in the hospital's ripple-bath. The lobotomy was an uneasy joke, not made any the funnier (or, for that matter, any the less serious) by casting an over-the-top comedian to play the surgeon.

There was a lyrical passage on Brooklyn Bridge when Samson escaped from the hospital and it seemed, just for a minute, as if he might do a Gene Kelly along the girders. It was a measure of Connery's success that the poet's boorish behaviour should have been so entertaining to watch.

72

Sean Connery in
A Fine Madness.

The lead is enthusiastically performed by Sean Connery, whose accent becomes more and more engaging with every film. When you hear him you can trace the story of his life, the glottal stop of metropolitan Scotland, the showbiz drawl of London, the Transatlantic snarl of New York. Without losing any of its origins the accent gets richer and more delightful in every new venture. Well directed, Connery attacks the part with eloquence. In one scene, imitating a man regressed to infantile idiocy, he is hilarious.

MIKE SARNE *Films and Filming*

If he wants to continue to be accepted as a serious actor, I suggest that he keeps out of comedy from now on.

LEONARD MOSLEY *Daily Express*

Sean Connery is an actor who often surprises with new turns of talent. As Samson he achieves something very rare in screen (or stage) personations of poets; you can feel that this bum actually *could* write a poem if he tried.

DAVID ROBINSON *The Financial Times*

Sean Connery is not the ideal actor for the role: the phlegmatic quality which makes him such a good James Bond inhibits him from complete identification with Samson's bull-in-the-china-shop view of life, and sometimes the film has the air of a great joke which no one has remembered to let its hero in on.

The Times

YOU ONLY LIVE TWICE

directed by Lewis Gilbert   1967

Sean Connery *is* James Bond, said the posters. As far as the public was concerned, it could just as easily have read the other way round. *You Only Live Twice* was better than *Thunderball*. The story-line was stronger, the action faster, the climax more explosive, and the sets by Ken Adams, especially for the secret hideout in a Japanese volcano, were even more spectacular.

There was plenty of exotic local colour: a wedding, a funeral, bathhouse massage, sumo wrestling, and a quick visit to the Ninja Commando School of the Japanese Secret Service, whose recruits are famous for their reflex actions and spiritual strength. The film did well at the box office and was good for the Japanese tourist industry.

The movie opened with Bond seemingly murdered in bed, having just made love. 'He died on the job,' said a colleague. 'He would have wanted it that way.' Buried at sea, and quickly resurrected, he was rewarded with a new toy, a baby helicopter with machine gun, rockets, and flame-thrower. The helicopter fight was one of the better sequences and there was also a good car chase which ended when Bond's pursuers were lifted off the road with a giant magnet and dropped into the sea.

As always the odds were overwhelming. He was often caught, but though the villains invariably threatened to kill him, they never ever did. They merely knocked him unconscious. It was the women, with whom Bond slept, who came to a sticky end: the lovely heroine (Akiko Wakabayashi) enjoyed a post-coital poisoning and the villainess (Karin Dor) was eaten by piranha fish, stripped to the bone in thirty seconds flat.

Donald Pleasence, in manic form, played Blofeld with a nasty scar. It was the first time in the series that SPECTRE's

Sean Connery and Akiko Wakabayashi in *You Only Live Twice.*

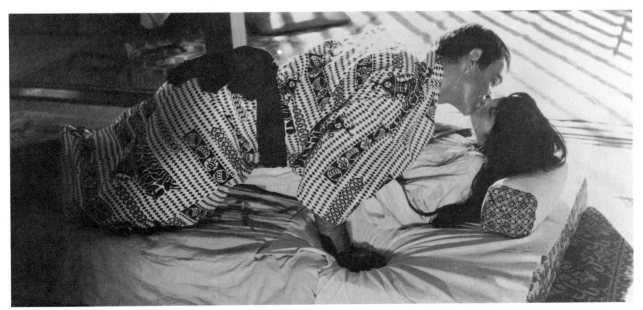

75

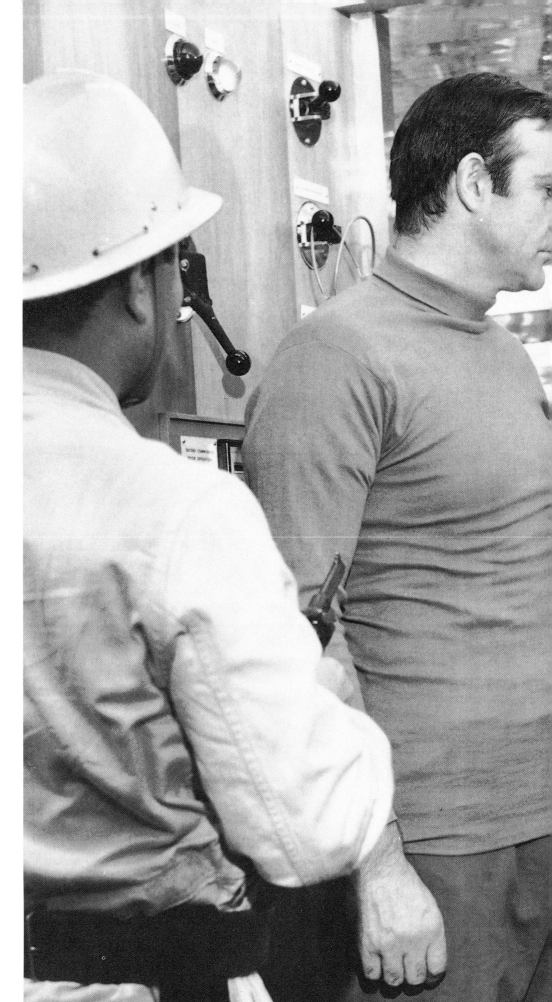

Sean Connery and
Donald Pleasence in
You Only Live Twice.

ugly face had actually been seen on the screen.

Sean Connery as Bond embarks on this latest suicidal mission with his usual cool detachment, and consolidates his image as the world's most perfect hero. His entertaining presence makes this platter of hokum the most delicious secret-agent yarn for months.

CLIVE HIRSCHHORN *Sunday Express*

The picture's saving grace is Sean Connery, who ambles through the proceedings with the cheeky contempt of an arts sixth former on a compulsory school tour of a nuclear station.

PHILIP FRENCH *The Observer*

Life as Bond now seems so uncomfortable (even the gallant Sean Connery begins to look haggard) that no one can really seek to identify with him. He's an institution, and as with many British institutions there's a distinct tendency to revert to the nursery – a brightly lit, shadowless place of pop art colours and painless death-dealing toys, with nanny M to blow the whistle at half-time.

PENELOPE HOUSTON *Spectator*

The Bond formula has now been run into the ground and only requires a headstone.

ALEXANDER WALKER *Evening Standard*

Bond, you are getting to be a bore.

ANN PACEY *Sun*

Above:
Sean Connery,
Mie Hama and
Tetsuro Tamba in
You Only Live Twice.

Opposite:
Sean Connery in
You Only Live Twice.

SHALAKO

directed by Edward Dmytryk   1968

In its way an historic meeting. Two of the great sex symbols of the age come to film.

Daily Mail headline

A party of European aristocrats were on a hunting safari in an Indian reservation in New Mexico in 1880. They behaved as if they were still in Europe and had brought along their furniture and silverware, plus a red-coated butler to serve chilled champagne. The producers went to great pains to insist that what looked like fiction was based on historical fact. There were moments, however, at the very beginning, when *Shalako* recalled *Carry On Up the Khyber* and that classic sequence of comic sang-froid in the face of marauding natives.

The party included an English lord and his lady, an arrogant German baron, a boring American senator, a French countess and their guide, an American white hunter. They were an unpleasant lot, cardboard villains most of them, with novelette dialogue and melodramatic looks to match, and the Indians, quite rightly, did not take kindly to their presence on their reservation.

Connery was cast as Shalako (the Apache word for Bringer of Rain), a former Confederate officer, who became their reluctant guide and attempted to lead the group to safety. There followed all the usual Western ingredients, including a fight with the Apache chief's son (Woody Strode), plus some lust in the hay and even a bit of rock climbing. There was plenty of action and most of it was dull.

Lady Daggett (Honor Blackman) chose

Sean Connery and Woody Strode in *Shalako.*

81

to start her affair with a renegade cowboy (Stephen Boyd) at the very moment the Apaches were attacking the fort. She deserted her husband, only to be caught by the Indians who murdered her by ramming her jewellery down her throat – easily the most dramatic moment in the movie.

Later there was an extraordinary picture of her husband, rifle in hand, advancing on the camera. Jack Hawkins went on advancing for so long, and so determinedly, that I thought he must be leaving the camp site and going after the Indians. In fact, he shot the cowboy ('At last I've managed to do something right'), but not before the cowboy had shot him. The butler (Eric Sykes) was then arrowed, presumably because his services were no longer required. Shalako and the countess rode off into the sunset.

The countess was played by an immaculate Brigitte Bardot in full riding habit and shiny top hat, sitting side-saddle, as if she were posing for a fashion plate in the Bois de Boulogne and Maurice Chevalier were about to sing 'Thank Heavens For Little Girls'. She had long blonde hair, white make-up and mascara-caked eyes. While waiting on top of a plateau for the 'injuns' to attack, she decided to have a wash in an icy pool and took off the top half of her dress for no good reason other than that cinemagoers expected the French actress to take something off. They were allowed a discreet look at her back as she clutched a towel to her bosom. 'You want me now?' she asked Shalako, who only minutes before had told her that most men had an instinct when a woman was available.

During the credit titles an over-lusty male choir sang about love coming to Shalako. Unfortunately, love did not come to Shalako until the closing moments (and then off screen), which was leaving it a bit late for most audiences. Connery was curiously colourless. On the other hand, there wasn't actually much for him to do except provide an intrepid presence until his good-humoured interlude with Bardot.

Shalako is our own Sean Connery, stepping into the well-worn boots of Cooper and Wayne as though they had been made for him.

PENELOPE MORTIMER *The Observer*

He is the best Western lead since the discovery of Steve McQueen.

ERIC RHODE *The Listener*

THE MOLLY MAGUIRES

directed by Martin Ritt   1969

Decency is not for the poor. You pay for decency, you buy it, and you buy the law, too, like you buy a loaf of bread.

JACK KEHOE

The Molly Maguires was set in Pennsylvania in 1876, among the Irish immigrant coalminers, seeking a better life. Scorned, exploited, persecuted, and living in what amounted to an armed camp, they were brutalised into submissiveness and defiant acts of violence.

The Molly Maguires was a secret terrorist organisation, an offshoot of the lawful Ancient Order of Hibernians, who got their name from the days when the young men used to disguise themselves as women. They had been terrorising the mining community for two decades, dynamiting and flooding mines and derailing trains. The sabotage was a protest against their working conditions, low pay, wretched housing and social discrimination.

The unseen management, represented by the forces of law and order (in the person of Frank Finlay), wanted to smash the organisation, and a detective (Richard Harris) was infiltrated into their ranks to catch them red-handed and thus bring enough evidence to hang them. The detective had decided the only way out of the poverty trap was to become an informer; but once he was disguised as a Molly, he became as brutal and as brave as any member of the gang, revelling in the looting and destruction.

Connery was cast as Jack Kehoe, the leader of the gang, a brave man yet a fool, who thought violence was the solution. The two men were alike, two sides of the

Anthony Zerbe, Sean Connery and Anthony Costello in *The Molly Maguires.*

Overleaf: *The Molly Maguires.*

same personality, and both were damned: one by the Catholic Church, the other by his act of betrayal. The detective, confused as to which side he was on, was the more complex, the more ambivalent character.

In an under-written role, Connery brought a brooding, sullen and bitter commitment to the cause. His performance was a striking portrait of a man suffering in silence, burning on the inside, keeping a tight rein on his emotions, until he let rip at the wake of an old miner, deeply angry that a man, who had spent his whole life in the mines, should have gone so quietly to his death and without even a decent suit to be buried in. Kehoe was determined that, before he died, he, at least, would 'make his sound, use his powder'.

The dialogue tended to be on the heavy side, lacking in clarity and humour. The poverty and squalor, on the other hand, had the authentic period feel of old photographs. There was also a memorable game of Gaelic football – harder and uglier than any bar-room brawl, and as dangerous – in which Connery and Harris were clearly seen to be taking part, alongside the professionals.

The Molly Maguires, sombre and elegiac, was based on real events and real people, and much of it was shot in the original locations, ravishingly photographed by James Wong Howe.

Sean Connery who has admirable screen presence – grace as well as strength – gives a sure and intelligent contrasting performance as the leader of the Molly Maguires, even though it is almost an unwritten role and we never discover what's in his head or how he thinks his explosions will feed his family.

PAULINE KAEL *New Yorker*

Connery proves that after years of James Bondage he is one of the screen's most underrated stars, an actor of tightly controlled power and technical accomplishment.

Time Magazine

Opposite and left:
Richard Harris and
Sean Connery in
The Molly Maguires.

89

LA TENDA ROSSA

directed by Mikhail Kalatozov   1969   English title: *The Red Tent*

Sean Connery in
La Tenda Rossa.

In 1928 General Nobile made his ill-fated airship expedition to the North Pole. Forty years later, when he was eighty-four years old, he imagined that the main participants were invited guests at a late-night party to present their views of what had happened and to argue about who was to blame for the failure. Should Nobile have left his men? Should he have allowed himself to be the first man to be rescued? The moral issues, raised by this phantom tribunal, never really came alive.

Connery, barely recognisable in a white-haired wig, made a late cameo appearance as Roald Amundsen, who lost his life in a vain attempt to rescue the marooned survivors. It was he who raised the question whether Nature wants man to conquer the Unknown.

Opposite:
Sean Connery in
*The Man Who Would
Be King.*

Peter Finch played General Nobile. The Arctic wastes were superbly photographed by Leonid Kalashnikov.

Most satisfying of all is Sean Connery's forgiving and understanding Amundsen, who has the last enlightening word in what I found a fascinating, if elementary, discussion of leadership, responsibility and heroism.
PATRICK GIBBS *The Daily Telegraph*

Connery as Amundsen is excellent, an intelligently drawn character study which represents his best work on screen since *The Hill*.
JULIAN FOX *Films and Filming*

90

The 1970s

THE ANDERSON TAPES

directed by Sidney Lumet   1971

Crime is the truth. Law is the hypocrisy.

DUKE ANDERSON

Duke Anderson (Sean Connery), an ex-convict, was longing to get back on the job, first with his girlfriend (Dyan Cannon) and then with the Fifth Avenue luxury apartment block, in which she lived, kept by her lover. His intention was to rob every single flat. As is always the case with the 'perfect crime' genre, the gang was less than perfect, and included a homosexual dealer in fake art (Martin Balsam, very camp), a junkie (Christopher Walken), a Black activist (Dick Williams) and a doddery old man out of prison for the first time in forty years (Stan Gottlieb).

What gave the story its originality and special interest was that the cops were on to Anderson's gang from the word go. The outside world was no different to the prison Anderson had just left. It was a world of closed-circuit TVs, tapped phones, electronic eyes, miniature transmitters, tape recorders, long-distance cameras, wall-defying earphones. Every word, every move was recorded.

Lawrence Sanders's novel, on which the script was based, consisted entirely of transcribed tape recordings and surveillance papers of the FBI, CIA, New York Police, Narcotics Bureau, Federal Trade Commission, private detectives, etc., etc. In the closing moments of the picture all the agencies were frantically erasing their illegal tapes, because if they didn't they, too, would be going to gaol.

The Anderson Tapes was a political satire on the paranoia of the United States. The irony was that since nothing was co-ordinated and everybody was working independently, nobody had the faintest idea what was going on and it was left to a paraplegic young lad (Scott Jacoby), working on his own with a short-wave

Sean Connery, Stan Gottlieb and Christopher Walken in *The Anderson Tapes*.

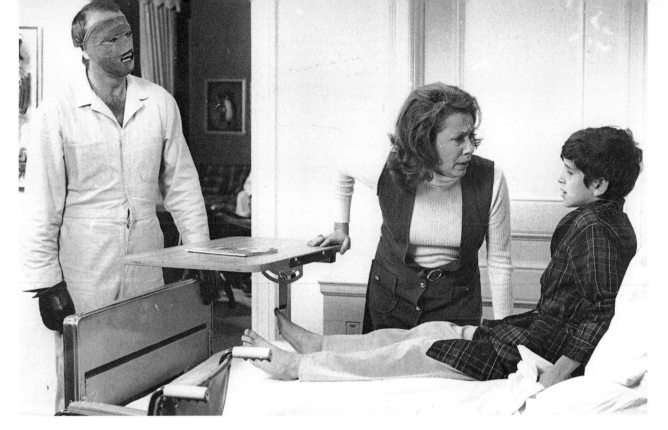

transmitter, to shame the professionals.

Sidney Lumet told the story crisply and efficiently, the action underlined by Clancy Jones's electronic soundtrack. While the burglary was actually taking place on the screen, Lumet leapt forward in time and intercut the sequence with the police questioning the victims *after* the event. There was some well-judged humour, which actually increased the tension, when a telephone operator refused to put through an emergency call to the police unless the call was paid for first. There was also a delightful cameo performance by eighty-year-old Judith Lowry as a little old lady, thrilled to bits that she was being burgled.

Connery, sullen and harassed, smouldering with rage at the ten years wasted in gaol, was the criminal as victim. He had a social conscience. 'What's advertising but a legalised con-game. And what the hell's marriage? Extortion, prostitution, soliciting with a government stamp on it? And what the hell is your stock market? A fixed horse race.' Dog ate dog and Anderson wanted the first bite.

Connery looks more substantial with every film he makes.

MARGARET HINXMAN *Sunday Telegraph*

Connery gives his best rough-diamond performance since his other great Lumet film, *The Hill*.

FELIX BARKER *Evening News*

The double infatuation with being a movie star and being James Bond has snapped Connery's powers as an actor both in terms of his plausibility and in terms of his technique. Casualness, which appears as an affectation in the Bond picture becomes a reality in the *Anderson* film. Since the latter is clearly unsatisfactory, one looks again at the former and concludes that probably the affectation is all that Connery is capable of. A harsh judgement maybe, but one arising out of the hope that beyond the low camp, a disciplined and tenacious actor still remains.

TONY PALMER *Spectator*

Sean Connery, Janet Ward and Scott Jacoby in *The Anderson Tapes*.

DIAMONDS ARE FOREVER

directed by Guy Hamilton   1971

Sean Connery and Jill St John in *Diamonds Are Forever*.

Diamonds Are Forever had some good things going for it, not least two silly chases. The first took place in the Nevada Desert, with Bond driving a twee lunar car; the second was up and down the Las Vegas strip, which ended with the police going round in circles, having a smashing time among themselves in the car park.

Women's Lib was represented by two Amazonian bodyguards, who gave Bond a really rough ride. There were also two gay assassins, fey yet quite ruthless, working hand-in-hand (literally). The couple were so funny it was surprising a Hollywood producer didn't resurrect them and give Bruce Glover and Putter Smith a series.

One thing you could be absolutely certain about in a Bond movie was that whoever got killed, Bond himself would only ever be knocked out. Agent 007 was immortal, even when he was locked inside a coffin which had been dispatched into the funeral furnace.

There was a good fight in a lift. The nastiest moment in the film came when Plenty O'Toole (Lana Wood) was thrown out of a window ten floors high. Fortunately for her, she landed in a swimming-pool. When the thug was congratulated on his aim, he pointed out, in that deadpan way so characteristic of the series, that he hadn't been looking where he had been throwing her. There

94

was also a typical Hitchcock touch when an Amsterdam guide was pointing out the tourist sites just as a body was being fished out of the canal.

As for Bond, he had put on weight. 'There is a lot more to you than I expected,' said the heroine (Jill St John). 'I'm on top of the situation,' he replied; and it wasn't long before he was.

Connery proves yet again that he is irreplaceable as Bond, handling the script's most worn *double entendres* like a master.

NIGEL ANDREWS *Monthly Film Bulletin*

Sean Connery returns to the role of Bond as bland as his admirers could possibly wish.

GORDON GOW *Films and Filming*

In a world that suddenly doesn't seem particularly worth saving, an aging Sean Connery invests Bond with a mellower brand of ruthlessness. He is suddenly more the gourmet and less the lecher, more the wanderer and less the hustler.

ANDREW SARRIS *Village Voice*

Connery, a fine, forceful actor with an undeniable presence, turns his well-publicised contempt for the Bond character into some wry moments of self-parody. He is capable of doing better *(The Molly Maguires, Marnie)* but whether he likes it or not, he is the perfect, the only James Bond.

JAY COCKS *Time Magazine*

Sean Connery makes a welcome return, and it's hard to believe the thing would work so well without his sardonic intelligence spraying scepticism over the corn.

GAVIN MILLAR *The Listener*

He no longer wears the waxy deadpan of a sex-fantasy stud dummy; over the years he has turned the robot matinée idol Bond into a man – himself. The foppery and the gadgetry have diminished, and the sexual conquests, too. Almost imperceptibly, Bond has lost his upper-class snobbery along with the toiletries; it's as if that snotty, enigmatic Bond disgusted Connery. His instinct was right: it's better this way . . .

PAULINE KAEL *New Yorker*

Bruce Glover and Sean Connery in *Diamonds Are Forever*.

THE OFFENCE

directed by Sidney Lumet   1972

Policeman: You bloody pervert!
Suspect: It takes one to know one.

The Offence opened in eerie, silent, slow motion to Harrison Bertwhistle's jarring and disturbing soundtrack. A man was discovered in a cell. A body lay on the floor. The police entered and they were attacked. But the man cinemagoers had assumed to be the trapped criminal, turned out to be a detective.

The film was an adaptation by John Hopkins of his stage play, *This Story of Yours*, which had enjoyed a critical success at the Royal Court Theatre in London. The play was a study of the mental and moral breakdown of a detective, brutalised by twenty years in the force, who had absorbed so much pain and suffering that he was no longer able to shut off at the end of the day.

Questioning a suspected child molester, he beat the man to death, seeing in him a mirror of his own paedophiliac desires, homosexual temptations, and innate violence. Early on the script raised the question whether the detective himself might not be the man the police were looking for. The scene, where he found the young girl in the woods, was deliberately ambiguous. Later, in a quarrel with his wife, when it seemed as if he might rape her, the quarrel was intercut with shots from the earlier scene with the child.

'Nothing I have done can be half as bad as the thoughts in your head,' said the suspect, who became (in Ian Bannen's wonderful performance) the policeman's tormentor. The actual moment when the roles of sadist and masochist were

Sean Connery in
The Offence.

97

reversed, and the policeman pleaded with the man to help him, was deeply upsetting. The suspect merely taunted him: 'You're pathetic! You sad, sorry, little man.'

Connery, abrasive and haunted, was very impressive as the detective, giving one of his most memorable perform-ances: a compassionate portrait, vividly drawn, of a crushed, sick man, frustrated by his unhappy marriage and lack of promotion.

Sidney Lumet handled the harrowing subject matter in a cold, stark, aggressive manner, never for one moment denying the theatricality of the confrontations between detective and suspect, detective and wife (Vivien Merchant) and detective and superior (Trevor Howard); yet his treatment, at the same time, was almost as concrete and documentary as *Z Cars*, while at others it could be almost surreal.

Connery has formidable attack and credibility as the policeman with dubious ethics.

VIRGINIA DIGNAM *Morning Star*

Sean Connery, liberated for once from action roles, conveys the sense of a man wracked by a terrible unseen destruction going on within him.

DAVID ROBINSON *The Financial Times*

Sean Connery's performance as the violent Scotsman, coarse-grained, obsessed, living – like Marlowe's Mephistopheles, in Hell – is beautifully played off against Ian Bannen's soft-spoken creepy rapist.

GEORGE MELLY *The Observer*

Above:
Sean Connery
in *The Offence.*

Opposite:
Sean Connery and
Ian Bannen in
The Offence.

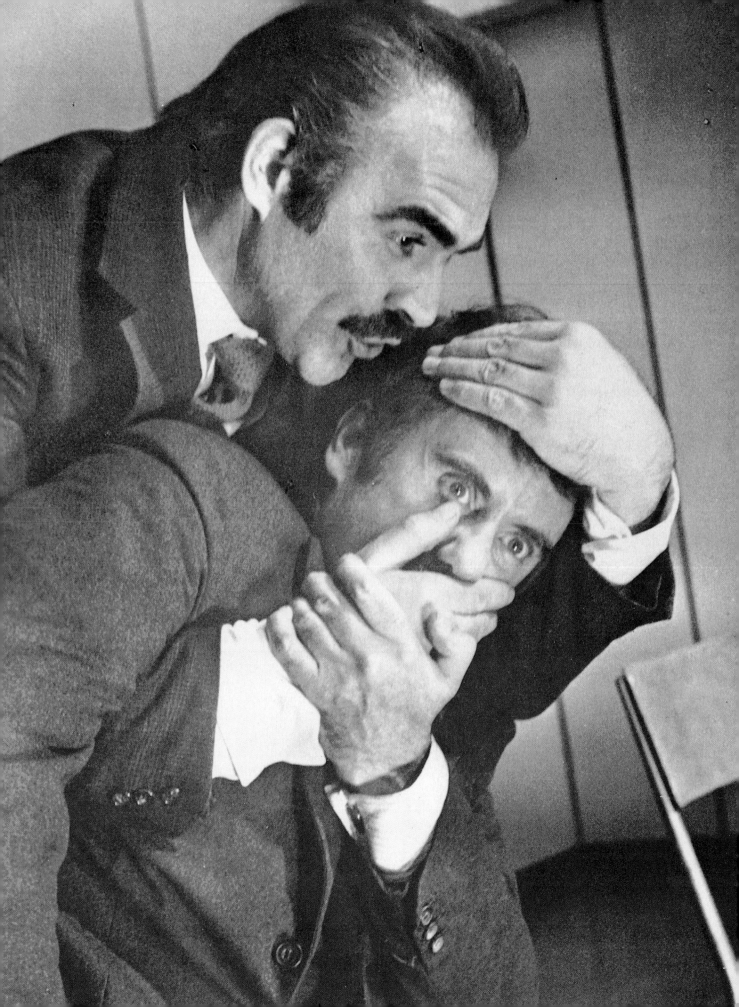

ZARDOZ

directed by John Boorman   1973

The gun is good. The penis evil.
Go forth and kill.

Z<small>ARDOZ</small>

John Boorman, who had just made a tremendous impact with *Deliverance*, promised cinemagoers a mixture of allegory and science fiction, a satirical film, full of mystery and intrigue, rich in irony. The new picture drew on Darwin, Tolkien, Swift, the Arthurian legend and the drawings of Blake.

Zardoz was a giant flying godhead, a stone boulder, spitting out rifles over a barren outland in 2293. He looked like the Magritte boulder in the sky, with a Mount Rushmore carving of a snarling Karl Marx for a face.

Zardoz was a fake god, invented by a technological commune of rich and powerful scientists and intellectuals, whose members had discovered the secret of eternal life, and lived in the fertile plains and valleys in their own sealed-off Vortex. The society was run by women, Eternals, super-intelligent, soulless, sexless women. Their men were Apathetics, impotent and effete. Anybody who objected to the system (a Renegade) was immediately rendered old and senile.

Connery was Zed, one of Zardoz's Exterminators, men of exceptional power, both mental and physical, who spent their days killing and raping, until Zardoz decreed there would be no more killings and the people would become farmers. When Zed discovered that Zardoz was a camp magician (a Wizard of Oz, in fact) he killed him and broke into the Vortex, bringing the commune an unbeatable

Sean Connery in *Zardoz*.

and much-needed package of sex and death. The Renegades, in the film's brutal and disturbing climax, greeted their massacre with joy.

There was not much for Connery to do but lend his considerable physical presence to the role. He made his first entrance, firing his gun straight into the camera, Boorman deliberately recalling a familiar logo. He was in excellent shape and wore very little – an orange loin-cloth, thigh boots, a bandolier of cartridges, a Mexican moustache, and his wig in a pigtail. Initially, he was a beast of burden and trotted around like an obedient super-stud.

Visually the film was often striking. The photography was by Geoffrey Unsworth. There was an extraordinary image of Zed acquiring the sum of all knowledge, the knowledge being superimposed on his body. There was another sequence, when he was trying to shoot his way out of a hall of mirrors, which paid direct homage to Orson Welles's *The Lady From Shanghai.*

Sean Connery in
Zardoz.

The crudest scene had the women in a seminar, studying the relation between stimulus and response, and giving Zed an electronic test to see what would give him an erection. They showed him various erotica, which had no effect whatsoever, and it was only when Zed looked at Charlotte Rampling (in her role as zoologist) that the cardiograph needle finally leapt to life.

Sean Connery plays him with a ferociously concentrated energy which imposes the character as both a physical and a moral force and does much to dispel one's doubts about the apparent loose ends in the philosophical tapestry.

JAN DAWSON *Monthly Film Bulletin*

Connery is very watchable, and as a version of the apocalypse it is better than any I've seen.

CHRISTOPHER HUDSON *Spectator*

Sean Connery in *Zardoz.*

RANSOM

directed by Casper Wrede   1974   US title: *The Terrorists*

Ransom, a study in brinkmanship, would have made good television. The British Ambassador to Scandinavia was kidnapped in his private residence and a plane was hijacked at the airport. The story-line proved difficult to follow, but the actual situation, told in quasi-documentary fashion, was gripping enough, with some good twists *en route* to the airport. The villains turned out to be the British Foreign Office.

Ransom was filmed in Norway, but since the Norwegians did not care for acts of terrorism to be taking place on their Tarmac, the country was called Scandinavia. The production was at its best when it kept its mouth shut. The dialogue tended to get very heavy-handed, especially in the scene where the Ambassador's wife was pleading with the airport security chief to save her sick husband. The confrontation became a stagey debate on the ethics of playing with hostages' lives.

Connery was cast as the uncompromising security chief, who was resolved not to capitulate to the terrorists' demands. Ian McShane was cast as the leading hijacker and Jeffry Wickham represented the FO.

Sean Connery and Ian McShane in *Ransom*.

Sean Connery always gives the impression of quiet strength. A good man in a crisis. But I always have the feeling that the screen roles don't extend him as they could. Since his charm-and-brawn performances as Bond, only his psychopathic detective in *The Offence* has given him a chance to get inside an interesting character. It is a pity, for when we meet I am aware of a thoughtful actor wanting to break out of the mould of the conventional he-man.

FELIX BARKER *Evening News*

Connery certainly deserves better than this.

CLIVE HIRSCHHORN *Sunday Express*

Ten years ago he was the world's No 1 box-office star. He not only laughed all the way to the bank — he bought it. But what of Sean Connery now? He walked away from Bondage saying: 'I want to make more movie subjects that will extend me as an actor.' Yet nothing has come up trumps since his last 007 stint. . . . There is nothing he can do, and he does very little. Throughout the whole affair he looked old, tired and browned out.

FERGUS CASHIN *Sun*

Knut Hansson, Sean Connery and Jeffry Wickham in *Ransom*.

105

MURDER ON THE ORIENT EXPRESS

directed by Sidney Lumet   1974

Murder on the Orient Express, a classic 1930s detective story, had one of Agatha Christie's most celebrated denouements, when it was discovered everybody had done it. Since the solution was all and the characterisation and the action nil, the production began with an arresting reference to the Lindbergh kidnapping and then put its trust in the star system (a star in every role) and the period fashions. The cast were given a magnificent cod-romantic entrance on a station platform filled with billowing smoke and a stylish curtain-call of clinking champagne glasses. The art deco designs were handsomely realised by Tony Walton.

Hercule Poirot (Albert Finney) exercised his grey cells while the famous actors sat around in a confined space, like so many glorified extras. Connery played Colonel Arbuthnot, a typical English army officer in plus fours, smoking a pipe and carrying golf clubs. He had just returned from leave on the North-West Frontier. It wasn't much of a part.

Jean-Pierre Cassel, Anthony Perkins, Vanessa Redgrave, Sean Connery, Ingrid Bergman, George Coulouris, Albert Finney, Rachel Roberts, Wendy Hiller, Denis Quilley, Michael York, Jacqueline Bisset, Lauren Bacall and Martin Balsam in *Murder on the Orient Express.*

THE WIND AND THE LION

directed by John Milius   1975

Morocco 1904. Raisuli, Sheriff of the Berbers (Sean Connery), kidnapped Mrs Eden Pedecaris (Candice Bergen), an American widow, and her two children. He offered to ransom her in exchange for money, rifles and sovereignty. President Theodore Roosevelt (Brian Keith), quick to seize a chance to improve his election prospects, issued an ultimatum ('Mrs Pedecaris alive or Raisuli dead!') and sent in the marines.

The film was based very loosely on a true incident. The first thing that John Milius's screenplay did, however, was to change the sex of the American captive so that the story could have not only lots of violence, but some good old-fashioned adventure and romance as well. The scene in which Mrs Pedecaris, her children and the Americans save Raisuli from the nasty Germans, was straight out of *Boys' Own*.

Connery's Raisuli, larger-than-life, gallant, courageous, acted with engaging self-mockery. 'The blood of the prophet is in me and I am but a servant of his will,' he would say, decapitating yet another head and rushing off to rescue the heroine single-handedly. He was the Lion, a proud man of integrity and honour, a legendary feudal lord, championing his right to rule in his own way, roaring defiance, because roar was all that he could do. Roosevelt was the Wind, free to go wherever he wanted. The two men never met, but they were kindred spirits, equally comic, especially when Keith (a Teddy-bear President) pretended to be the grizzly bear he had shot, and posed for the taxidermist.

Connery's and Bergen's performances owed something to Bernard Shaw's *Captain Brassbound's Conversion* (he playing Brassbound to her bossy Lady Cecily Waynflete) and something to *Anna and the King of Siam* and Rudolph Valentino's *The Sheik*. The romance was strictly platonic. Connery looked magnificent, but he sounded awful. The accent was incongruous and the dialogue banal and stilted.

Milius approached his subject in the manner of David Lean, even using the same locations as *Lawrence of Arabia*. The action scenes were best. The spectacular scenery was beautifully photographed by Billy Williams, who made a guest appearance, dying, defending Mrs Pedecaris, in the exciting and brutal kidnapping sequence (brilliantly edited by Bob Wolf), which got the film off to a tremendous start.

The later attack by the marines, arriving on the double at the Banshaw's palace, was no less brutal, though the brutality was somewhat deflated by Vladek Sheybal's Banshaw, who merely expressed camp irritation at the massacre going on all around him.

In a bravura performance, Sean Connery captures the fierce nobility of the desert warrior to perfection, adding a mischievous sexuality to his strictly platonic encounters with Mrs Pedecaris, whom Candice Bergen delightfully invests with a similar spirit.

RICHARD BARKLEY *Sunday Express*

Opposite:
Sean Connery in
The Wind and The Lion.

109

There is also a performance by Sean Connery to rank among his best, considering that the role is among the clichéd worst.

TOM HUTCHINSON *Sunday Telegraph*

As a Welshman, I'm all for the Celtic comeback, but not in Arab costume. It wouldn't be so bad if Connery's mien were generally moderate, but Milius has persuaded him to exude a carefree, laughing *joie de vivre* which puts an almost Goonish slant upon the role: it's the mad Sheikh of Aberdeen, folks.

RUSSELL DAVIES *The Observer*

In particular, Connery brings his part off well, suggesting a man of dignity as well as audacity – a benign tyrant with a proud past but a sense of proper foreboding about the future.

DEREK MALCOLM *Guardian*

He and his Arabs give the impression of a stranded touring company of *The Desert Song* waiting to get the show on the road.

ARTHUR THIRKELL *Daily Mirror*

I wasn't sure whether Sean Connery's character was meant to be as funny as it seems.

KENNETH ROBINSON *Spectator*

Candice Bergen and Sean Connery in *The Wind and The Lion*.

THE MAN WHO WOULD BE KING

directed by John Huston   1975

They have two-and-thirty heathen idols there, and we'll be the thirty-third and -fourth.

PEACHEY CARNEHAN

John Huston had been wanting to film *The Man Who Would Be King* for twenty years. The original idea had been to cast Humphrey Bogart and Clark Gable in the roles now played by Michael Caine and Sean Connery.

The story, set in the 1880s, described two ex-soldiers' hazardous journey from India to Kafiristan, there to make their fortunes and become emperors of the earth. 'India's not big enough for us,' they said. Rudyard Kipling's ironic parable on imperialism, written when he was twenty-two, was a rousing yarn for those who hankered after the British Empire, the Raj, jingoism and racism. Huston's film, shot on location in the Atlas Mountains of Morocco, had an epic sweep.

Sean Connery and Michael Caine, as the inseparable rogues, Daniel Dravot and Peachey Carnehan, mates-to-the-death, were an amusing double act, a

Opposite and below: Sean Connery in *The Man Who Would Be King*.

couple of music-hall comedians, out of
the barrack-room poetry of Kipling, and
up to all sorts of antics, like smuggling,
swindling, blackmailing, gunrunning,
Freemasonry and training the warring
tribes how 'to slaughter their enemies like
civilised men'. The natives, admittedly,
were a barbaric lot and played polo with
the decapitated heads of vanquished
rulers.

Connery and Caine, nicely contrasted,
acted with their tongues firmly in their
cheeks. 'It was detriment like us that built
the bloody Raj!' The larky working-class
banter was very enjoyable. Caine dominated the first part of the movie;
Connery, the second.

Connery had the more difficult role
when Dravot actually came to believe in
his own myth, first imagining himself as

Opposite and above:
Sean Connery in
*The Man Who Would
Be King.*

115

another Alexander the Great, and then thinking he was a god. When his bluff was finally called at his wedding and it was clear to the priests in the Holy City that he was not a god (gods don't marry mortals), Dravot turned tragic hero and went to an unforgettable singing death on a severed rope bridge, strung across a ravine. He took, said Peachey in that awesome line, half an hour to fall till he struck the water.

Christopher Plummer was excellent as Kipling and there were delightful performances by Doghmi Larbi as a cowardly chieftain and Saeed Jaffrey as a devoted ex-Gurkha, faithful to the British Empire to the last, sacrificing his life in a parody of a brave yet futile gesture.

With the glorious exceptions of Brando and Olivier, there's no screen actor I'd rather watch than Sean Connery.

PAULINE KAEL *New Yorker*

But it is Connery who continues to be amazing. With every film he grows in stature, discarding all vestiges of James Bond – which never sat too easily with him – to become a truly fine character actor.

MARGARET HINXMAN *Daily Mail*

Dravot calls for intricacies of character-isation, and obtains them from Sean Connery, good as he has ever been and perhaps at his very best, juggling with our guarded sympathy and our escalating ridicule.

GORDON GOW *Films and Filming*

Saeed Jaffrey,
Michael Caine and
Sean Connery in
*The Man Who Would
Be King.*

116

ROBIN AND MARIAN

directed by Richard Lester   1976

I'd never have written a piece about
Robin if I weren't moved to tears by
aging heroes and their swan-songs.

JAMES GOLDMAN

The working title for the film had been
The Death of Robin Hood, but the studio
preferred a more commercial title, and
inevitably sent out all the wrong romantic signals to its potential audience.

Richard Lester looked at the legend
afresh, not only celebrating it, but
commenting on it as well. Robin Hood,
disillusioned by the crusades ('a damn
fool's errand') and sickened by the
atrocities Richard the Lionheart had
committed in the Holy Land and else-
where, returned to England's green and
pleasant land (filmed in Spain) to pick up
where he had left off twenty years before.

James Goldman's theatrical script,
which mixed frivolity with high serious-
ness, was in his colloquial *The Lion in
Winter* vein, full of self-conscious
twentieth-century irony and anachron-
ism. For a moment, at the very beginning
when a catapult failed to shoot its
boulder, it seemed we were in for the
larkiness which had informed Lester's
The Three Musketeers and *Royal Flash*; but
though there were jokes, the vision this
time was much bleaker and the mood
more elegiac. The heroism and romance,
of a classical love story, were seen within
a more realistic context. The film, badly
underrated by most critics, was on a par
with *The War Lord* and *El Cid*.

Connery, grey-bearded, balding, arth-
ritic, bruised and scarred, was no jolly
agile Douglas Fairbanks. Rather was he

Audrey Hepburn
and Sean Connery
in *Robin and Marian*.

118

the Robin of the original ballads, the rough-hewn peasant bastard, who could not resist a good fight, a tragic flaw, which would finally be his undoing. Connery was a Robin for the 1970s, as charismatic as ever and still a potent masculine symbol, but stripped of his courtly tradition, capable of knocking Marian out, and a little in love with death, teasing the Grim Reaper. He knew his legend was fiction, but, like everybody else, he was caught up in it, vainly attempting to regain his youth and the old excitement by reliving past exploits.

Audrey Hepburn, making her return to the screen after a seven-year absence, played Marian, now turned abbess. 'I've never kissed a member of the clergy,' said Robin. 'Would it be a sin?' Evidently not, since she removed her wimple and they adjourned to make love in the cornfields. Hepburn had both an outer and inner beauty and their sentimental reunion was gentle and touching.

Robert Shaw's arrogant yet canny Sheriff of Nottingham was a worthy adversary. Sharp, dangerous and intelligent (far more intelligent than Robin), he bided his time. Their fight to the death had none of the panache and elegance of the rapier thrust and parry of Errol Flynn and Basil Rathbone. What Lester offered was something more brutal: the sight of two worn-out warriors, barely able to lift their heavy swords, clumsily hacking at each other. Robin killed the Sheriff, but was himself mortally wounded. Marian, declaring that she loved him more than God, poisoned them both to provide a stagy, tear-jerking climax.

Richard Harris and Sean Connery in *Robin and Marian.*

Sean Connery and
Robert Shaw in
Robin and Marian.

Richard Harris made a splendid Richard the Lionheart and Ian Holm offered a neat cameo of mad King John.

Connery now – big, fleshy, graying – is the most natural-looking of heroic figures. He seems unrestrained, naked: a true hero.

PAULINE KAEL *New Yorker*

Connery has become peculiarly adept at playing ragged, restless period adventurers (and the liability of his Scots accent is ingeniously reduced by making all the other outlaws sport one).

GEOFF BROWN *Monthly Film Bulletin*

Connery, in particular, has never been given his due as a straight actor, and if anyone is responsible for keeping the potentially flabby scenes between him and Miss Hepburn from wilting, it is he.

GAVIN MILLAR *The Listener*

THE NEXT MAN

directed by Richard C. Sarafian   1976

Middle-East tensions. Oil millionaires. Spies. Terrorists. The film opened with two people being thrown out of a window while a London busker danced to a jaunty tune in the street below.

Connery (who, as usual, did nothing to change his accent) was cast as the Saudi Arabian Minister of State, who was described as a great man coming out of the desert, looking to the future and ignoring the past. His vision made him many enemies. Three Arabs, who had wanted to break the United States/Soviet Union stranglehold, had already been murdered. So when, at the United Nations, he declared his intention of leaving OPEC and proposed a partnership with the State of Israel, it was clear to everybody that he was the next man on the list.

In the circumstances, his behaviour was extraordinary. His Excellency, who combined high politics with high living and some cooking, proceeded to fall in

Sean Connery and Cornelia Sharpe in *The Next Man*.

123

love with his freelance assassin (Cornelia Sharpe) and was amazed when she shot him dead in a New York traffic jam. Yet only the day before he had been shown watching King Kong toppling off the Empire State Building, on late-night TV, and still not taking the warning. As any movie buff could have told him, it wasn't the aeroplanes that got Kong. It was Beauty killed the Beast.

There was a sequence in the Bahamas, which served merely as a travelogue interlude, providing local colour, water-skiing and native dancing in the streets. When the action finally came, it was regrettably straight out of a Bond movie and His Excellency suddenly, and ludicrously, turned 007.

Connery walks through the film with flair and convincing dignity.

Film Bulletin USA

Above and opposite: Sean Connery in *The Next Man*.

A BRIDGE TOO FAR

directed by Richard Attenborough   1977

The party is on and no one is going to call it off.

A Bridge Too Far was the story of the Battle of Arnhem, in September 1944 during World War II, and described the airborne assault behind the German lines in Holland, the biggest operation since D-Day.

The war might well have been over by Christmas, had not bad weather, poor intelligence, faulty radios, ill-chosen landing sites and logistic problems screwed everything up. There was a complete breakdown of communication. Nobody knew what the hell was going on. It was a disastrous shambles from start to finish, and a costly failure in life.

The film, daunting in its complexity and scale, patriotic in its music, modest in its acting, was both a tribute to courage and a tragic record of folly, waste, incompetence and futility. It benefitted enormously from its documentary approach and the audience's hindsight. The battle scenes were excellent. Particularly moving was the massacre of the Americans, saying their Hail Marys as they paddled frantically across the swirling, bullet-strewn river. The final image, of the wounded and dying singing 'Abide With Me', might have been a scene from Richard Attenborough's *Oh! What A Lovely War.*

A Bridge Too Far was said to have had the most expensive cast in living memory. There were famous actors everywhere, a battlefield of well-known names, and much was made of the staggering amounts some of them were earning. A Star Too Many, said the wags.

The international cast included Dirk Bogarde, James Caan, Michael Caine, Elliott Gould, Gene Hackman, Anthony Hopkins, Hardy Kruger, Laurence Olivier, Ryan O'Neal, Robert Redford, Maximilian Schell and Liv Ullmann. Edward Fox, in his role of Lieut. General Horrocks, was immensely likeable when he was driving down a seemingly never-ending road of stationary vehicles and men, hailing his officers with a quip as he passed them.

Connery was cast as General Urquhart, the commander of the airborne troop, in his first combat drop. His was one of the most substantial parts in the film. Told by 'Boy' Browning that Montgomery was proud and pleased, Urquhart glowered with disbelief and anger. Pleased? He had gone in with ten thousand men and come out with less than two thousand. Connery was there to give the story its full moral force and he did exactly that.

Opposite:
Sean Connery in
A Bridge Too Far.

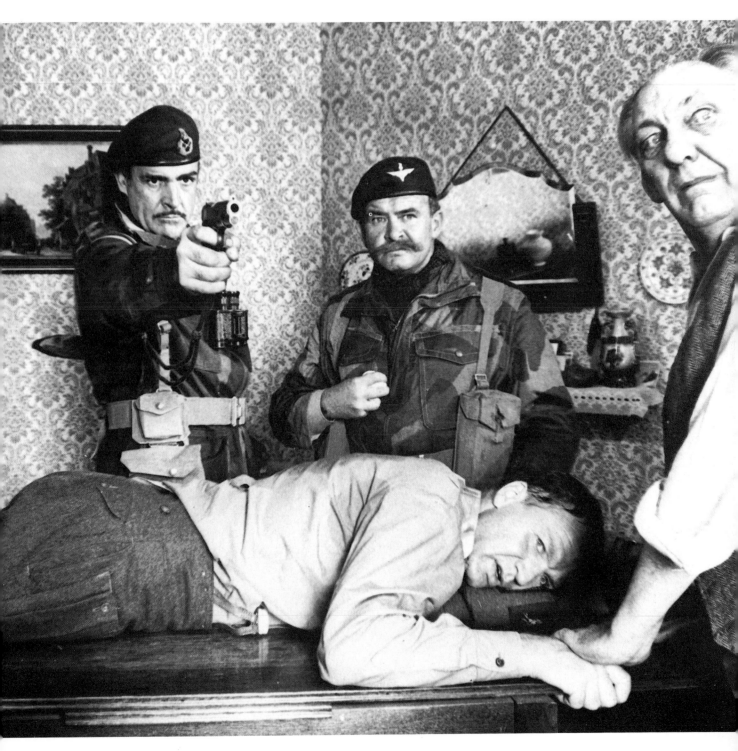

THE FIRST GREAT TRAIN ROBBERY

directed by Michael Crichton   1978   US title: *The Great Train Robbery*

Judge: Why did you commit this
       scandalous and dastardly crime?
Crook: I wanted the money.

The film, set in the 1850s, was a handsome, fast-paced and facetious account of the theft of gold bullion from a train, running from London to Folkestone, on its way to pay the troops in the Crimea.

Robbers did not crack safes in those days. Since dynamite and combination locks had not yet been invented, they could only open them with keys. The actual stealing, of the four keys to the two safes without their owners knowing, was great fun; one of the thefts involved a seventy-five-seconds sprint at a railway station while the watchman was absent from his post.

Connery, whiskered and in a stovepipe hat, was the gentleman-crook, suave, insolent, cynical, worldly and charming with the anachronistic sexual innuendoes, which gave a period story a contemporary touch. Feeling, as always, that a double dilutes the quality of the

Donald Sutherland and Sean Connery in *The First Great Train Robbery*.

performance, Connery did his own hair-raising stunt work, running along the top of the moving train, ducking bridges as he went.

Donald Sutherland played his partner-in-crime, a master cracksman and pickpocket. Lesley-Anne Down played his mistress and Wayne Sleep played the cat-burglar who escaped from Newgate Prison to join the gang.

Victorian England, its Dickensian slums, prisons, banks, mansions, clubs, pubs and bordellos were brilliantly recreated in Dublin. The film was dedicated, with love and respect, to the brilliant photographer, Geoffrey Unsworth, who had recently died. He had worked with Connery on *Hell Drivers*, *Murder on the Orient Express*, *Zardoz* and *A Bridge Too Far*.

Sean Connery and Lesley-Anne Down in *The First Great Train Robbery*.

Sean Connery is a most engaging rogue.

Arthur Thirkell *Daily Mirror*

Connery's cool rogue occasionally conveys a bit of Crichton's original intentions. The character's honest amorality stands in contrast to the false piety of the wealthy bluebloods he swindles.

Frank Rich *Time Magazine*

Above:
Sean Connery in
The First Great Train Robbery.

Opposite:
Wayne Sleep and
Sean Connery in
The First Great Train Robbery.

METEOR

directed by Ronald Neame   1979

Meteor was a disaster movie, long past its sell-by date. A giant meteor, five miles wide, hurtled towards earth. The devastation was expected to be equal to ten thousand hydrogen bombs. The only way the planet could be saved was by American and Russian scientists working together to shoot the meteor down with their combined nuclear rockets.

The cliché-ridden script remained earthbound and the special effects (apart from an avalanche) were simply not special enough to make up for the lack of imagination. The rockets never left the drawing-board; and as for the meteor, it looked like diarrhoea in the sky.

Connery was cast as a top NASA scientist, who found time to fall in love with a Russian translator played by Natalie Wood. Brian Keith was the friendly Russian scientist.

Henry Fonda, who was cast as the President of the United States for the third time, had a situation not unlike the one he had played in Sidney Lumet's excellent *Fail Safe* in 1964. Many critics thought he made a much more convincing President than Ronald Reagan.

Meteor would lose to a firework display on a very rainy night.

DEREK MALCOLM *Guardian*

See it on peril of death by boredom.

TOM MINE *Time Out*

Brian Keith,
Natalie Wood and
Sean Connery in
Meteor.

134

CUBA

directed by Richard Lester   1979

A political film within which no one spoke about politics and a love story in which no one spoke about love.

RICHARD LESTER

Cuba, an unconvincing mixture of realistic documentary and cliché-ridden romantic melodrama, was a mess, though not nearly as dull and ridiculous as was made out when it concentrated on the guerilla warfare and the Christmas massacre rather than the romance.

The scene was Havana, 1959, on the eve of a revolution; the time, the last two weeks of the corrupt Batista regime. Connery was cast as a British mercenary, a retired British army major, who believed in democracy: 'I would never use a gun against a legitimate government,' he declared. Nevertheless, he was a bit dubious about his present role, which was to act as security adviser and train the Batista army to stop the Castro rebels.

He met up with an old girlfriend (Brooke Adams), now married to a philandering alcoholic, and the big, boring question was whether she would leave her husband and fly to safety with him. The last reel played like a parody of *Casablanca*.

Any woman who would pass up Sean Connery (he is in terrific shape here, in a trim tan business suit and a narrow fedora) in order to keep her white wide-wing Cadillac convertible deserves whatever fate the insurgents plan for her.

ROGER ANGELL *New Yorker*

Danny de la Paz, Brooke Adams, Sean Connery and Jack Watson in *Cuba*.

Danny de la Paz and Sean Connery in *Cuba*.

Some of it is so ludicrous I wondered whether it was originally conceived as a comedy. As a British soldier of fortune engaged to stiffen Batista's army Sean Connery wanders around looking understandably perplexed.

MARGARET HINXMAN *Daily Mail*

Mr Connery, who has saved worse films than this, has his work cut out here.

DAVID CASTER *Sunday Telegraph*

Opposite: Sean Connery in *The Untouchables*.

The 1980s

TIME BANDITS

directed by Terry Gilliam   1981

He had just the right twinkle, the right amount of authority. Everything's there. We wanted a hero and Connery's a hero.

TERRY GILLIAM

Time Bandits was a comedy-fantasy-adventure for children, with an occasional nod in the direction of their parents. An eleven-year-old lad (Craig Warnock) journeys through history and mythology, in the company of six robber-dwarfs, meeting some of his favourite heroes, including Napoleon (Ian Holm), Robin Hood (John Cleese, very Pythonesque) and King Agamemnon (Sean Connery, very benign).

The main reason for seeing the film would have been for Terry Gilliam's visual flair and spectacular technical tricks. There was a memorable shot of a giant rising out of the sea, directly under a galleon, and striding to shore with the ship still on his head. The dwarfs, led by David Rappaport, had the most fun. The rest of the cast, which included Ralph Richardson (in his own crumpled suit) as God, and David Warner as the Devil, played a supporting role to the special effects.

There wasn't much for Connery to do. He wore a splendid helmet, killed the Minotaur, waved to the crowds, and watched an indifferent entertainment.

The Minotaur, speaking at a press conference in Crete, after the film's premiere, said that reports of his death by Agamemnon were grossly exaggerated. Theseus was unavailable for comment, still lost in the corridors of the Palace at Knossos.

Opposite and left: Sean Connery in *Time Bandits*.

OUTLAND

directed by Peter Hyams   1981

Outland was *High Noon* in the sky, a marriage of science fiction and Western, with Connery in the Gary Cooper role of marshal.

On Io, the third moon of Jupiter, a year's travel from Earth, a titanium mining company was breaking all records in production. At the same time, there had been a record outbreak of suicides and psychotic attacks. The new marshal, with the aid of the company's woman doctor, discovered that the miners were being given an illegal drug, which increased their output for eleven months and then drove them insane. The marshal determined to break the drug racket. The company determined to break him and hired two assassins. The marshal went along to the local brothel: 'I could use a little help,' he said. He found no volunteers, except the doctor, played by Frances Sternhagen, acid-tongued, raddle-faced, hard-drinking and tough as old boots.

The technology was impressive, but the characterisation was patently weak. There were hints of troubles in the marshal's past, of his having been too arrogant and outspoken, and wanting now to find out about himself and see if he was man enough to do it alone. But none of this was properly scripted and developed. He was merely a one-man crusade, a decent cop fighting the system. There was none of the vulnerability and sheer fear which had made Cooper's marshal so real. The final showdown took place in outer space, in insulated suits and oxygen masks and tubes, which robbed the actors of all personality.

The claustrophobic set, with its towering complex construction of steel (designed by Philip Harrison with acknowledgement to the Dodge cities of the past and the oil rigs of the present) provided a dramatic setting for the film's best sequence, a chase among the girders, excitingly photographed and edited by Stephen Goldblatt and Stuart Baird respectively. The chase ended in the kitchens, with Connery's head in the frying pan.

Opposite and below: Sean Connery in *Outland.*

140

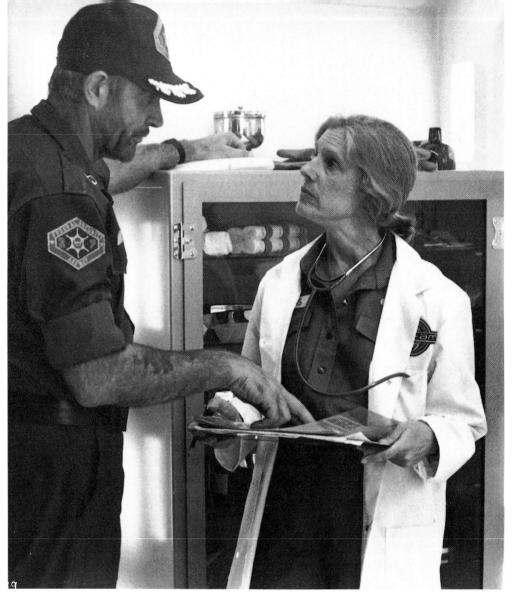

Sean Connery and
Frances Sternhagen
in *Outland*.

Connery is perhaps the one genuine
romantic hero in the movies now. He is
strong; he is soft. He can be hurt
physically, and take it; he can be hurt
emotionally, and show it.

RICHARD CORLISS *Time Magazine*

Through clenched molars, uttering
well-shaped lines at a soft clip, he again
demonstrates his uncanny power of
investing dialogue with subtle
personality. Hardly moving a muscle,
except to hit someone, he seems to
express the grizzled intelligence of the
entire film and its feelings, too.

DAVID HUGHES *The Sunday Times*

Connery, with his curl-lip grin and
flinty grace, lends nearly all the weight

there is to this near weightless plot.

NIGEL ANDREWS *The Financial Times*

Don't go. Give it a miss. Avoid it like the
plague. Tell your friends to pass it by.
The acting is bad, bad, bad (Sean
Connery as a grizzled space sheriff
included).

CHRISTOPHER HITCHENS *New Statesman*

Sean is an extraordinary actor, and he
has that rare quality, his emotions seem
very close to the surface of his skin. You
have the impression when you
photograph him, that you can truly
sense what he's feeling. He has a very
powerful image on screen, and he's a
tremendous craftsman.

PETER HYAMS

THE MAN WITH THE DEADLY LENS

directed by Richard Brooks   1982   US title: *Wrong Is Right*

What happened to the American image?
How did America become a dirty name?

The American title was so much better. *The Man With The Deadly Lens* merely suggested a James Bond movie, which it wasn't, but which, no doubt, was the intention after the film's failure at the box office in the United States.

The script was a cynical satire on the power of the media. Kings, presidents, politicians and terrorists all paid court to television, because 'if it doesn't happen on television, it doesn't mean a thing'.

Connery was the television reporter/newscaster/anchorman as superstar, always there in the thick of the fighting, bringing the violence, as it happened, into people's homes. He was both a crusader and a cynic. 'Violence is what the nation wants. Violence is the national pastime. Violence is commercial. Violence is good for the ratings. We're in the entertainment business!'

The President of the United States was tricked by the CIA into authorising an assassination which had already happened. He was then forced to go on to television and justify his homicide, on the lines that if it was good for America, then what he had done could not be wrong. In the meantime, two atom bombs were for sale on the open market, and he was told that if he didn't resign, Jerusalem and New York would be destroyed. The film ended with the President declaring war (a sure-fire election winner) and Connery throwing away his toupée.

Richard Brooks, confused as to what the film was meant to be, attempted to be

Sean Connery in
The Man With The
Deadly Lens.

143

all things to all audiences: political satire, paranoid thriller and nuclear disaster movie. His targets included US imperialism, CIA intervention, Islamic fundamentalism, media technology, mad generals and keep-fit presidents. The result was frenetic. It was like watching a marriage of *Dr. Strangelove* and *Network*.

The most terrifying and unforgettable moments were those in which men and women, having been injected with explosives, detonated themselves at public meetings: human bombs as a television spectacular.

Sean Connery has never been so admirable as when he bestrides this exploding farrago of death and destruction like a colossus, making James Bond seem like Roger Moore.
ALAN BRIEN *The Sunday Times*

As an investigative journalist working for a US television network, Sean Connery is ill-at-ease, mouthing sententious platitudes about media responsibility, while negotiating a labyrinth plot and encountering at every junction an actor or an actress performing in a totally different style.
PHILIP FRENCH *The Observer*

You may well laugh all the way to the holocaust.
ARTHUR THIRKELL *Daily Mirror*

Sean Connery in *The Man With The Deadly Lens.*

FIVE DAYS ONE SUMMER

directed by Fred Zinnemann   1982

The characters are sketchy. It was not the characters in the short story that interested me but the story's final situation.

FRED ZINNEMANN

Fred Zinnemann, at seventy-five, was still haunted by Kay Boyle's *Maiden Maiden*, a short story he had first read three decades earlier. He had always wanted to film it in black and white, feeling that colour would sentimentalise the mountain setting and not do justice to the 'lost silence' he remembered so vividly from the days when he, as a young man, had gone climbing in Switzerland.

A middle-aged Scottish doctor (Sean Connery) and a young woman (Betsy Brantley) were on a climbing holiday in the Swiss Alps. It seemed at first that they were father and daughter; then it seemed as if they were on their honeymoon; finally, it was revealed they were, in fact, uncle and niece, and that they were having an affair.

During a climb the doctor and his niece discovered the dead body of a man who, forty years earlier, had gone missing on his wedding day. His bride had never married. Now a little old lady, she was brought face to face with her groom, his youth having been miraculously preserved in ice all those years. It was a poignant reunion without words. This tragedy from the past inevitably presaged a new tragedy.

The niece, who had had a crush on her uncle since she was a child, knew better than he did that their affair was doomed, and resolved to stay on after he had returned to Scotland. The truth was that she had fallen in love with their young Swiss guide (Lambert Wilson). The two men became undeclared sexual rivals and sought to win the maiden by conquering The Maiden, the most difficult peak in the area. There was an accident and one of them fell. The question was which one.

This gentle, potent parable felt like a television drama, stretched by unnecessary flashbacks. There was little dialogue; so little it could have been a silent film. Indeed, the shot, of the niece's necklace breaking and the beads scattering all over the floor, was a once-classic way of suggesting sexual congress without disturbing the censor. Similarly, the final scene, with the couple trudging endlessly towards each other, was the very stuff of which melodramas were made in the silent era.

The story unfolded at an unhurried pace and it said much for the actors that their sensitive performances were not completely dwarfed by the magnificent scenery and nerve-racking climbs. The colour photography by Giuseppe Rotunno was breathtaking. The actual filming of the body falling, shot in three long takes, was stunning, and the fact that it obviously was a dummy (what else could it be?) did not make the shot any the less stunning.

Connery saw the doctor as a sort of Ibsen figure, a pillar of the community, ruled by his darker emotions. He was most moving in his vulnerability, subtly conveying the guilt beneath the surface.

Opposite:
Sean Connery and
Betsy Brantley in
*Five Days One
Summer.*

Lambert Wilson, Betsy Brantley and Sean Connery in *Five Days One Summer.*

But Zinnemann's masterstroke is to cast Sean Connery as the doctor. Connery's grim, almost impenetrable manner has seldom been used so effectively: he seems as stoic and monumental as the mountains themselves, even though he has almost been undone by his own emotion.

RICHARD COOK *New Musical Express*

In the hands of Sean Connery, in the smile, the wrinkled eyes, the thoughtful brow – yes, even in the balding head of Sean Connery, the man has a visible seasoned sex appeal. What a wonderful actor he has aged into.

ALEXANDER WALKER *Standard*

SWORD OF THE VALIANT – THE LEGEND OF GAWAIN AND THE GREEN KNIGHT

directed by Stephen Weeks   1983

Sword of the Valiant was a remake of *Sir Gawain and the Green Knight*, which had also been directed by Stephen Weeks, and had flopped in 1972. The roles, originally taken by Murray Head and Nigel Green, were now played by Miles O'Keefe and Sean Connery. The film flopped again.

Sir Gawain and the Green Knight, written in the last quarter of the fourteenth century, is a sophisticated and civilised work, though you would never have guessed it from this adaptation, cheaply made, poorly acted, and uncertain in its approach and continuity. Even the sword was tacky.

Connery, bare-chested, robust and wild, looked good in his green wig, shaggy beard and antlers. This was more than could be said for Gawain, who looked merely silly in his pantomime blond wig.

The film seems so amateur; almost grotesque enough to pass as a substandard offering from a struggling local amateur dramatics group.

PAUL REES *Western Mail*

Sean Connery and Miles O'Keefe in *Sword of the Valiant*.

NEVER SAY NEVER AGAIN

directed by Irvin Kershner   1983

Good to see you, Mr Bond. Now you're on to this, I presume we are going to have some gratuitous sex and violence.

Agent 007 was now all of fifty-three, and hadn't been on the job for twelve years. M decided he had better be on the safe side and packed him off to the health farm. Here, in a sequence which was both exciting and hilarious, he was pursued and very nearly killed by a giant maniac, demolishing everything in his path. There was nothing, absolutely nothing, which was capable of stopping the man, until Bond, in desperation, having thrown everything else at him, picked up a specimen of his own urine and threw it in his face. That stopped him.

The story was the usual terror and extortion, with Blofeld (the ultra-smooth Charles Gray) still wanting to destroy the world. This time the ultimate nightmare was the theft of nuclear warheads. The heroine was played by Kim Basinger, a cool tango-dancing blonde. Barbara Carrera was a cartoon *femme fatale*, a praying mantis in a boa, swishing about in flamboyant costumes and high-heeled shoes, clickety-clicking down stairs in high camp style. Best of all was Klaus Maria Brandauer, who had scored a brilliant success in Istvan Szabo's *Mephisto*. He brought a welcome subtlety to the crazy villain: a magnetic, chilling performance, and charming and sexy with it, too. It was disappointing that his final confrontation with Bond, in a vulgar video game, which gave electric shocks to the loser, should have been so singularly lacking in invention and thrills.

Sean Connery in *Never Say Never Again*.

150

Kim Basinger and
Sean Connery in
*Never Say Never
Again.*

Nevertheless, despite the generally sluggish direction, especially in the boring final section in an Egyptian temple, *Never Say Never Again* was one of the better Bond films, and certainly vastly superior to *Thunderball,* which it recycled, sharks and all.

It's good to see him back in action, for Connery has lost none of his charm and, if anything, is more appealing than ever as the stylish resolute hero.

IAN CHRISTIE *Daily Express*

Connery has brought back the world of adult fun which made the earlier Bond movies so compulsive – a fun, like the best Christmas panto jokes, balanced on a knife's edge between naivety and knowingness.

NICK RODDICK
Times Educational Supplement

There is a bullish edge of menace to his characterisation even, perhaps especially when he flashes his sharkish smile. Most important, he is unapologetic about the unlikable facets of 007: in other hands these have been allowed to soften in ingratiating flippant comedy. It's the first time in a decade that the Bond films have had a new feel and a new look: and Mr Connery is double-OK.

DAVID CASTEL *Sunday Telegraph*

Above all, there is the undeniable pleasure in watching Connery traverse the part again, effortlessly suggesting both the arrogance the part needs and the sly humour without which it could so easily become unbearable. Welcome back.

DEREK MALCOLM *Guardian*

HIGHLANDER

directed by Russell Mulcahy   1986

Highlander, an urban swashbuckling thriller, was a sixteen-million-dollar epic fantasy adventure, switching back and forth from the highlands of sixteenth-century Scotland to twentieth-century New York.

The story came from a film student at the University of California. The director, a brash new talent, all technical pyro-technics, came from the world of music video and pop promotion. The film had plenty of visual energy. The highlight of the production was a tremendous bravura fight in an underground garage beneath Madison Square Garden, the actors leaping on cars, to an accompaniment of flashing lights, smashing car bonnets, exploding windshields, bursting live steam pipes, and activated overhead sprinklers. The soundtrack was loud and the special effects were a knockout. There were also striking shots of Glen Nevis, Glencoe and Loch Shiel.

Christopher Lambert, French heart-throb, star of *Subway* and *Greystoke: The Legend of Tarzan, Lord of the Apes*, played the shaggy Highlander, Conner MacLeod, who had problems coming to terms with being immortal. Born in 1518, mortally wounded in battle in 1536, MacLeod lived on, to the distress of his clan who drove him out of the village. Four and a half centuries later he was wandering round New York, decapitating rivals with a magnificent Japanese sword, pursued by the villain, the police and the authoress of *A Metallurgical History of Ancient Sword Making*.

While making love with Heather in the Scottish heather ('You can do that to me for ever if you like, my lord.'), MacLeod was interrupted by Ramirez (Sean Connery), who had been born 2437 years earlier in Egypt and was at present Chief Metallurgist to Charles V of Spain. He explained to MacLeod that he was one of a unique breed of men who only died when they were decapitated. Ramirez (a magnificent peacock given to self-mockery) became his tutor and taught him how to save mankind, with art, faith and steel, until he himself lost his own head to evil Kurgan (Clancy Brown, hoarse of voice and coarse of acting), who

Sean Connery in *Highlander*.

thought it better to burn than fade away.
Connery had panache.

For his brief time on screen, Mr
Connery brings dash and style to the
overblown proceedings.
WALTER GOODMAN *New York Times*

Why should someone like Sean
Connery get himself involved in
something as nasty and inane as
Highlander?
BENNY GREEN *Daily Mail*

Connery, however, is terrific and made
me at least wonder why his long career
has included little or no swashbuckling,
because here he manages a mature
Errol Flynn to great effect as a terrible
senior time lord.
WILLIAM RUSSELL *Glasgow Herald*

Christopher
Lambert and
Sean Connery in
Highlander.

DER NAME DER ROSE

directed by Jean-Jacques Annaud   1987   English title: *The Name of the Rose*

All that remains of a dead rose is its name.

HERBERT DE ROUBAIX

Umberto Eco's *The Name of the Rose* was a terrifying murder mystery set in a remote and forbidding Benedictine monastery in northern Italy during the fourteenth century. Not the least of its many terrors – and these included a dead body in a barrel of pigs' blood, a bloated dead body in the bathhouse, the burning of heretics and the impaling of an Inquisitor on the spikes of a wheel – was a labyrinth library out of Escher.

Eco, a world-famous specialist in semiotics (who, incidentally, had made a structuralist study of James Bond), had originally called his novel *The Abbey of the Crime*, but changed it, fearing the public might think it was merely a medieval whodunit. Nevertheless, the fact that *The Name of the Rose* was a multi-layered, scholarly, erudite work did not stop it becoming an international best-seller, translated into twenty-four languages.

Jean-Jacques Annaud has described his film as a palimpsest, which, as everybody knows, is a manuscript on which the original text has been rubbed out and another written on top. The novel's metaphysical content might have been diluted, but the visual impact, a marriage of Federico Fellini and Hammer Horror, remained very powerful. Tonino Delli Colli's photography and lighting made reference to Vermeer, Rembrandt, Caravaggio and Giotto.

Annaud, who had gone to inordinate lengths for historical accuracy, in every prop, every piece of furniture and every book, searched Europe for fifteen of the most extraordinary-looking actors to play the monks, and returned with an international gallery of Gothic grotesques, to delight Bosch and Bruegel, faces and bodies so gnarled and distorted as to frighten, not only the Hunchback of Notre Dame but the gargoyles as well. The only homely face was that of the Abbot, played by Michel Lonsdale, the French actor billed, rather strangely, as Michael Lonsdale.

In the library, one of the greatest libraries in Christendom, was the last copy of a Greek manuscript on comedy by Aristotle, which was the key to the murders. But what could be so alarming about laughter? The answer, according to the old and blind librarian (Feodor Chaliapin, Jr.), was that laughter killed fear and that without fear of the Devil there was no need of God.

The crime was solved by William of Baskerville, a visiting Franciscan monk from England, who had come to attend a conference and discuss whether the Church should accumulate wealth for the glory of God or whether it should celebrate poverty. Baskerville, a twentieth-century detective in a fourteenth-century habit and cowl, was a role once earmarked for Michael Caine.

Connery, his love of learning and books transparent, brought to the part enormous spiritual authority and intellectual pride. He was a sturdy and manly symbol for reason and justice in a world of ignorance and superstition, personified by the Inquisitor (F. Murray Abraham, acting in capital letters), a

Opposite:
Christian Slater and Sean Connery in *The Name of the Rose.*

character as sinister as his black carriage and black horses.

Baskerville was accompanied by Adso of Melk, a young novice who played Watson to his Holmes. 'My dear Adso, it's *elementary.'* Actually, there were moments when Baskerville, a kindly, compassionate father-figure to his acolyte, sounded more like Hercule Poirot; and certainly in one bit of editing, the film borrowed directly from the Agatha Christie movies.

Sixteen-year-old Christian Slater played the wide-eyed novice, seduced by a mute peasant, the lad's first and last sexual experience. The film was awarded an 18 certificate, which presumably meant that Slater wasn't allowed to see himself *in flagrante delicto.*

Sean Connery,
Michael Habeck,
Christian Slater and
Eya Baskin in
The Name of the Rose.

Sean Connery gives one of his best performances. Craggy and composed, he exudes a tremendous quiet authority. Better still, he manages quite brilliantly to convey a fascination with intellectual inquiry, by no means an easy thing to do.

WILLIAM PARENTE *The Scotsman*

Connery radiates presence, even in grey sackcloth, spicing the Gothic horror with a sardonic twinkle.

SHAUN USHER *Daily Mail*

Connery almost makes chastity appealing (you think that if *he's* into it, there must be something to be said on its behalf).

DAVID DENBY *New York Magazine*

THE UNTOUCHABLES

directed by Brian de Palma   1987

Let's do some good!

ELIOT NESS

The time was 1930, the Prohibition era: spats, fedoras, Lloyd Wright buildings, and tommy-guns. *The Untouchables* was a stylish period piece which gave a fictional account of the events leading up to Al Capone's arrest for tax evasion, no other charge sticking. It was a subject Brian de Palma had already touched on in *Scarface*, a remake of the 1930s classic.

Rival gangs in Chicago were competing for the city's billion-dollar empire of illegal alcohol. Enter Eliot Ness (Kevin Costner), the inexperienced and incorruptible special agent of the Treasury Department. He picked his own men, the mobsters having already bribed the mayor, government officials, judges, and, of course, the police. The team included an Irish cop (Sean Connery), an Italian American sharpshooter (Andy Garcia) straight out of police academy, and a middle-aged, myopic government accountant (Charles Martin Smith), who enjoyed himself hugely until he got murdered in a lift, one of de Palma's more chilling set pieces.

Al Capone was not amused by Ness. 'I want you to find this nancy boy. I want him dead. I want his family dead. I want his house burned to the ground. I want to go there in the middle of the night and I want to piss on his ashes.' Robert de Niro, wearing (so it was reported) the same silk underwear Capone used to wear (though cinemagoers never got round to seeing de Niro in his underpants), gave a grandiloquent, manic performance, a caricature of an already

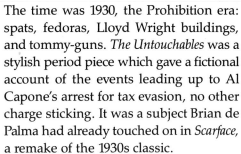

Charles Martin Smith, Kevin Costner, Sean Connery and Andy Garcia in *The Untouchables.*

161

Sean Connery and
Kevin Costner in
The Untouchables.

over-the-top villain, who was pretty adroit with a baseball bat at the dinner table.

Ness, an idealistic family man, quickly lost his innocence, and realised that evil could be stopped only by evil. 'I have broken every law I swore to defend. I've become what I've beheld and I'm content that I have done right.' At one stage he unexpectedly turned cowboy and took the violence off the streets and into the countryside, with an ambush, helped by the Canadian Mounties.

Malone, the honest Irish cop, still walking the beat in his old age, had a beat-wise philosophy: 'Make sure,' he said, 'when your shift is over, you go home alive. Here endeth the lesson.' Malone was gruff, tough, pragmatic, his face registering years of experience. There was a gun in the gramophone, a bottle of whisky in the stove and a St Jude medal in his pocket. St Jude is the patron saint of the police and lost causes.

The cop's relationship with Ness was the backbone of the film. Tutor, mentor, friend, maverick, Connery was a forceful, knowing counterweight to Costner. Rugged yet gentle, tough yet tender, he brought to the role an Old Testament eye-for-an-eye justice.

Malone's death scene was as melo-dramatic as anybody could have wished,

the tension maintained by tracking shots down the long corridor of his apartment, filmed from the view of the assassin hunting him. Malone, his body riddled with bullets, crawled to his death down the corridor, coughing, groaning, leaving a trail of blood. The distraught Ness leant over the dying cop, crying, 'STAY! STAY! NO! NO!' Cinemagoers might have been participating at a performance of some Italian opera. Indeed de Palma wittily punctuated the whole scene with Pagliacci singing *Vesti la gubba*, while Capone sat in a private box, weeping his heart out, until his hit man told him Malone was dead.

The hit man (Billy Drago, excellent) wore a white suit and ghoulish make-up, a cartoon-like figure to complement his boss. Ness finally gave him the push, off the Court House roof. Hitchcock would have approved.

The film's climax took place on the marble staircase in Union Station and paid homage to one of the cinema's most famous sequences – the steps of Odessa in Eisenstein's *The Battleship Potemkin*. In the deserted station Ness waited to arrest Capone's bookkeeper. While he was waiting, he helped a mother carry her pram up the stairs. The mobsters arrived just as they were nearing the top of the stairs. The moment the shooting began,

162

all human sound was cut, the soundtrack concentrating only on the gunfire and the sound of the pram bumping down the stairs. The whole sequence, in slow motion, was brilliantly edited by Jerry Greenberg and Bill Pankow.

Connery won an Oscar for best supporting actor.

Sean Connery's fine performance as Malone provides the film with its moral center.

JANET MAILIN *New York Times*

Sean Connery invests Malone, the veteran patrolman whose help Ness enlists, with more authority than the part deserves.

JOHN GROSS *New York Times*

Connery, perhaps the least acceptable macho actor, brings a sinewy force to his work, but his lines are blustery and conventional.

DAVID DENBY *New York*

Few actors but Connery, however, could make credible the metamorphosis, with his promotion to be Ness's lieutenant, from a cynical old-on-the-beat cop to a kind of gangland Flash Gordon.

DAVID ROBINSON *The Times*

Equating Chicago with gangsters is like expecting to see gladiators and Christians when you go to Rome.

D. CLANCY, Executive Director, Chicago Tourist Council

Sean Connery and Kevin Costner in *The Untouchables*.

THE PRESIDIO

directed by Peter Hyams   1988

Rick Zumwalt and
Sean Connery in
The Presidio.

A murder took place at the Presidio, an historic military base in San Francisco, near the Golden Gate Bridge. The military police (in the person of Sean Connery's Provost-Marshal) and the civilian police (in the person of Mark Harmon's detective) worked in reluctant tandem to solve the crime. The Provost-Marshal had once been the detective's CO and had him busted. The detective had never forgiven him.

There were scenes of action, including a *Bullitt*-like car chase by night and another chase on foot through Chinatown, down streets, down alleys, through kitchens, through windows and over cars. In between there was love-making and dreary sentimental talk.

'I have known buildings that are easier to talk to than you,' said a wartime buddy (Jack Warden) in a heart-to-heart on a very stagy roof-top. 'I've lost her. She hates me,' moaned the Provost-Marshal, referring to his wayward daughter who was having an affair with the detective to spite him. Since the detective was also having an affair to spite his former CO, the couple had a good time.

The emotional relationships were as artificial as the clashes between the two adversaries. Harmon was brash. Connery was grizzled. Neither was likeable. There was a scene where Connery, tough, beat up a lager-lout in a pub; and there was

Mark Harmon and
Sean Connery in
The Presidio.

another scene where Connery, tearful, delivered a funeral oration. Both scenes were out of character.

As for the murder plot, which was impossible to follow, it had something to do with smuggling and blackmail by Vietnam war veterans. The climax was a ridiculous shoot-out in a water-bottling plant. *The Presidio* was strictly for people who didn't go to the cinema and stayed at home and watched videos.

Connery has given up pretending to talk English. That Edinburgh burr is back on the front desk, without apology. His qualities as an actor are so subtle and consummate that the smallest gesture is enough. He adds authority.

ANGUS WOLFE MURRAY *The Scotsman*

INDIANA JONES AND THE LAST CRUSADE

directed by Steven Spielberg   1989

> You get all the action that you had in the first Indiana movie, plus an emotional experience in the relationship between Indiana and his father. This is what gives the film its edge.
>
> HARRISON FORD
> quoted by LESTER MIDDLEHURST *Today*

There were old maps, old castles, codes, secret passages, revolving panels, exotic travel, deserts, mountains, canyons, snake pits, a sewer of rats, a lion, storms at sea, tombs, buried treasure, and lost cities, half as old as time. All this and the Nazis, and Hitler, too. The film smashed box-office records and deserved to. *Indiana Jones and the Last Crusade* was a wonderfully absurd and entertaining 1930s schoolboy adventure story, told with verve and humour.

'There's no way out!' cried a villain, who clearly had not seen the previous two *Indiana* films. Indy, a romantic and cynical adventurer in leather jacket and fedora plus bullwhip, was a modern-day knight in search of the Holy Grail, the cup that held the wine at the Last Supper and Christ's blood after the Crucifixion.

The action sequences – in cars, aeroplanes, trains, speedboats, tanks, zeppelin and on horseback – had all the technical prowess and panache audiences had come to expect from a Steven Spielberg movie. The pace was fast and the stunts, an integral part of Indy's character, were breathtaking. But what made the film extra special was that this

Harrison Ford and Sean Connery in *Indiana Jones and the Last Crusade.*

166

time, Indy took his dad along with him. The relationship between the cantankerous father and his son, the son he hardly talked to for twenty years, worked a treat, the mild sparring and mutual antagonism giving way to bemused affection when he started to enjoy his son's adventures. The sentimentality and the innuendo were perfect. 'I am as human as the next man,' said Dad, bookish maybe, but still sexually active, apologising for having slept with the spy who had betrayed them. 'I was the next man,' said the disconcerted Indy.

Connery exuded scholarship, his

Sean Connery and Harrison Ford in *Indiana Jones and the Last Crusade.*

characterisation modelled in part on the Victorian eccentric, Sir Richard Burton. With his beard, in his tweeds and trilby, and carrying a bulging attaché case and old 'brolly' everywhere, he was everybody's caricature of a professor. Yet at the same time, Connery was totally acceptable as a serious archeologist, an authority on the Holy Grail, immersed in his work, quick to rebuke his son for his blasphemy. His obsession and his faith had an inner strength, absolutely essential if the film's difficult final minutes were not going to be silly.

Connery and Harrison Ford were a

marvellous team. Connery was also totally believable as Ford's father, though there were only eleven years between them, Connery being fifty-eight and Ford forty-six.

As played by Sean Connery, he is a wonderful creation, part pawky Glaswegian comic-turn, part stern Caledonian Calvinist patriarch, a cross between Harry Lauder and Lord Reith.
PHILIP FRENCH *The Observer*

Harrison Ford and Sean Connery in *Indiana Jones and the Last Crusade*.

James Bond has finally met his offspring.
JONATHAN KING *Sun*

Ford brings strength of character to everything he does. Connery brings wit and a powerful presence. Together they work miracles.
ANGUS WOLFE MURRAY *Scotsman Weekend*

Connery's twinkle-eyed, crinkly-smiled authority lends the film what little nobility it has.
NIGEL ANDREWS *The Financial Times*

FAMILY BUSINESS

directed by Sidney Lumet   1989

We needed someone irresistibly charismatic so the audience would believe that a very bright young man might perceive him as a romantic role model.

LAWRENCE GORDON, Producer

Given the cast and the director, *Family Business* was a big disappointment. A thief (Sean Connery) had brought up his son (Dustin Hoffman) to be a thief. The son, having been to prison, decided to go straight and became an honest meat-packer, sending his own son (Matthew Broderick) to college. The bright lad dropped out, wanting to follow in Grandpa's footsteps. Crime was in his genes.

The grandson had a brilliant idea: a million-dollar burglary of a laboratory from which they would steal some test-tubes and a log-book. It was not only easy, it was foolproof. Granddad was all for it. Father was not, but came along to look after his boy. The burglary went wrong and the grandson was arrested. Should he languish in jail for fifteen years and the family sell the plasma and formula and make a fortune, or should Dad own up and send himself and Granddad to prison?

The robbery was momentarily funny when the grandson got lost, and momentarily exciting when he set off the alarm without realising he had done so. But as for the rest, the script was very talky, very mawkish and slackly plotted. And since the blood ties were all-important, it was a bit hard to understand

Dustin Hoffman,
Sean Connery and
Matthew Broderick
in *Family Business*.

Opposite:
Dustin Hoffman and
Sean Connery in
Family Business.

Matthew Broderick, Dustin Hoffman and Sean Connery in *Family Business*.

how Granddad could be Scots, the father Sicilian and the son Jewish.

Granddad, who had his own dubious code of morality, believed that crooks were far more straightforward than honest people and that so long as a risk was involved, the crime was OK. 'If you can't do the time,' he said, 'don't do the crime.' It seemed, therefore, only right and proper that this veteran robber, who had spent a lifetime in gaol and had no regrets, should die in a prison infirmary.

Family Business ended with a roof-top wake and his ashes being blown over the city, while the assembled guests, which included family, crooks, nuns and cops, sang 'Danny Boy'.

Everything he does is so well-honed that you can forgive the film almost anything.

DEREK MALCOLM *Guardian*

Connery gives a wonderfully infectious impression of the sexagenarian rogue, scoffing at his son's bourgeois existence and commanding the respect of citizen and cop alike as a 'class act'. A fair description, too, for this unusual caper movie.

JOHN COLDSTREAM *Sunday Telegraph*

And only Connery, voice burring and features a-twinkle with Celtic mischief, rises above the carnage like the buoyant superstar he is – astonishingly, at 59 – becoming.

NIGEL ANDREWS *The Financial Times*

Much as one respects Connery, one is beginning to wish he had never been awarded the Oscar for *The Untouchables*: it is as though directors are now feeling themselves obliged to indulge his every hammy mannerism. The entire film is a criminal waste of talent which leaves a slightly unsavoury after taste.

ANNE BILLSON *Sunday Correspondent*

Opposite: Sean Connery in *The Russia House*.

The 1990s

THE HUNT FOR RED OCTOBER

directed by John McTiernan   1990

The whole mystique of submarines is that you simply don't know where they are or what they're doing. A submarine is a hunter and the question is always who's doing the hunting and what is being hunted.

TOM CLANCY

Connery, maverick and capable of murdering the KGB officer with a single blow, was always totally in command, acting with stealth and authority, and speaking the occasional line in Russian.

Opposite:
Sean Connery in
The Hunt for Red October.

Below:
Sean Connery and
Alec Baldwin in *The Hunt for Red October.*

Tom Clancy's Cold War novel, an international best seller, sold six million copies. By the time the movie came out, the Cold War was over. The producers merely prefaced the film with a statement to the effect that the story was set in 1984, before Gorbachev came to power.

The Hunt for Red October was based on a real incident. A renegade Soviet submarine commander (Sean Connery), a Lithuanian by birth (not so out-of-date after all), hijacked the prototype of a virtually undetectable Soviet nuclear submarine, so silent as to be inaudible to sonar. The Soviets wanted to destroy it before it fell into enemy hands. The Americans, uncertain of the captain's motives, and fearing a nuclear strike, also wanted to blow the vessel out of the water. A CIA analyst (Alec Baldwin) was convinced that the captain wanted to defect. He was given three days to prove his theory. Who would get to Red October first? The film was another *Fail Safe* situation.

Baldwin was likeable and credible until the script turned him into a schoolboy hero, and had him absurdly steering the Russian submarine, while the captain stood by giving him the odd instruction. Later, he had to flush out a saboteur all on his own.

175

John McTiernan directs Sam Neill and Sean Connery in *The Hunt for Red October*.

I had tried to treat the film as a piece of entertainment, rather than as a piece of geopolitics or political philosophy – I basically tried to take the politics out of it.

JOHN MCTIERNAN

Connery brings all his customary presence, charisma and dignity to the role of Raimus but he is not actually called upon often to do anything. So he stands around looking like Sean Connery in a fetching uniform and a silver wig.

NEIL NORMAN *Evening Standard*

Connery's the lynch-pin, of course, shrewdly cast as the dour, wily captain. It's a fine less-is-more performance, full of repressed emotion, sardonic humour.

SHAUN USHER *Daily Mail*

He is the only real reason to see this long-winded adaptation.

DEREK MALCOLM *Guardian*

THE RUSSIA HOUSE

directed by Fred Schepisi   1990

How do you know who the decent people are?

John le Carré's familiar subject, spying and double-crossing, was given an additional twist by being set during a time of *glasnost* and *perestroika*. However, though there might have been a new openness, nothing had changed. It was the same old intrigue, as complex and over-elaborate as always, though not as thrilling as it used to be in the days of the Cold War.

The theme ('If there is to be hope we have to betray our country') was established immediately when a dissident Soviet scientist (the excellent Klaus Maria Brandauer) smuggled a manuscript to the West. The manuscript disclosed that the Soviet nuclear threat was bogus and that the West was in danger only from Russian lies.

Fred Schepisi directs Sean Connery in *The Russia House.*

Opposite:
Sean Connery and
Michelle Pfeiffer in
The Russia House.

The CIA (represented by Roy Scheider) and MI6 (represented by James Fox) sent a publisher to check the authenticity of the manuscript. They didn't want to believe it was true. Like their Soviet counterparts, they lived off the Cold War and wanted the arms race to go on for ever.

The publisher, Barley Blair (Sean Connery), was a bluff, boozy, incorrigible old cynic, who looked (so he said) like a large man-made bed. Blair actually loved Russia and its people, and was most reluctant to be lured into the spy game. There was a witty scene when he was put through his paces by the CIA, and took them for a ride, seemingly giving them the correct answers. He said he had been brought up to despise liberal opinion by his father, which was just the sort of thing the CIA wanted to hear, until he added that his father had been a hardline communist. Asked if there were any anarchists among his jazz acquaintances, he admitted there had been one trombone player (pause) who was not an anarchist. The script was by Tom Stoppard.

Blair arrived in Russia, met the courier (Michelle Pfeiffer), and fell in love with her. Their romance was observed from two perspectives, alternating between the audience's vision in the cinema and the vision of the Anglo-American spymasters back home, using all their sophisticated surveillance hardware.

Blair, finally, had to act like a hero in order to be a human. Faced with a choice between honour and ideology, he chose honour and defected to live happily ever after in Lisbon. The story ended in gooey sentiment, the reunion of publisher and courier replayed in slow motion.

The Russia House marked the first time that a major American company had been allowed to film in Russia. The most striking use of location was the shot of what seemed to be an art gallery, until a train ran through it, for this was Moscow's underground with its sculpture, mosaics and chandeliers. But the image, like so much of the location work, was used for itself rather than to advance the story dramatically.

Sean Connery revels in Barley, relying on the roguish charm of a man born to be free.

ANGUS WOLFE MURRAY *Scotsman Weekend*

Connery is as relaxed as ever, and we get lots of that curly Celtic smile. What it betrays is not just Barley's high spirits as he plays the spooks at their own game, but Connery's sardonic ease at yet another joshing part. His unrivalled solidity as an actor needs to be spiced with menace or urgency, as in *Marnie* and *The Name of the Rose*, or even the better days of Bond. Schepisi thinks he's got a complex character on his hands with this disillusioned dipso, but handles it far too cosily to let any of that come through, taking the hero's side against the twits without a murmur.

ANTHONY LANE *Independent on Sunday*

Sean Connery and
Klaus Maria
Brandauer in
The Russia House.

Connery is currently enjoying an Indian
summer of stardom, and he invests this
role with his usual wry charisma. Few
actors can have fought so long and so
hard against type-casting, and there
must be a particular pleasure in playing
a part so precisely opposed to the
bugbear Bond, one who chooses 'real
people' over 'unreal secrets'.

ADAM MARS-JONES *Independent*

HIGHLANDER II – THE QUICKENING

directed by Russell Mulcahy   1991

The time was 2024 and the world was dying. There was no sun, no stars: only heat and humidity. It had something to do with the ozone layer. The story was terrible. The action was all visual effects and mindless violence. *Highlander II*, hugely expensive, was nothing like as good as the original.

'When you need me you have only to call my name.' Juan Villa-Lobos Ramirez was quite a name to yell if you were in difficulties. The Spanish grandee, who had died in *Highlander*, was resurrected and Connery made a number of entrances to a bagpipe accompaniment. He interrupted a performance of *Hamlet* and visited a tailor, trying to inject some humour into the film. He was embarrassingly unfunny. The best joke was an inflight safety video, and that felt like an incongruous clip from *Airplane!*

'Will I ever see you again?' asked the immortal hero (Christopher Lambert). The answer was almost certainly yes. Michael Ironside was a splendid villain, with a manic grin which made him look like Jack Nicholson's Joker in *Batman*. He took commuters for a crazy ride on the subway. The commuters, many of whom had already seen *The Taking of Pelham One Two Three*, were hysterical.

A jocular appearance by Sean Connery is the main bright spot in the orange peasouper visuals and murky plot.

SHEILA JOHNSTON *Independent*

Not even Sean Connery can save it.

TOM HUTCHINSON *Mail on Sunday*

Sean Connery in *Highlander II.*

181

MEDICINE MAN

directed by John McTiernan   1992

It is not difficult to see what might have attracted Sean Connery to *Medicine Man* in the first place. The theme is both the environment and health. Here is a story about the destruction of the rainforests and a search for a cure for cancer. What is not so clear is why he, in his role of actor and executive producer, accepted the script with its awful dialogue and clichéd situations.

Dr Robert Campbell (Connery in shorts, his hair in a pony tail) is a brilliant, unorthodox research scientist who has gone native deep in the Amazonian jungle. Just as he is on the verge of a major medical breakthrough, the university decides to cease funding the project and sends a woman (Lorraine Bracco, from the Bronx with accent to match) to tell him their decision. Her arrival leads to an instant and highly-manufactured battle of the sexes along the lines of *The African Queen*. The chemistry, however, remains strictly in the test-tubes. Connery practises a bit of golf.

John McTiernan is much more interested in the possibilities for romance and adventure than he is in the politics. So there is much swinging about between trees on ropes and pulleys (the actors visibly doing their own stunts) to a musical accompaniment by Jerry Goldsmith which is so over-the-top you wonder why Hollywood never turned Tarzan and Jane into a musical. There is an episode where the heroine nearly falls to her death and has to be rescued by the hero. The whole thing is so artificially contrived, and so unexciting, it would have been far more in character (and funnier) for him to have left her to save herself, hanging there on her back on a branch suspended 300 feet over a gorge.

There is a scene where Campbell has to fight with the Indian medicine man. He is said to be in danger of having his skull cracked open, but the danger never for one moment exists. There is also a scene of gratuitous violence where he is beaten up, more appropriate to *Predator* and *Die Hard*, and there is another sequence, equally gratuitous, when the camera pans back and forth along a line of naked Indian female buttocks.

He provides the only hint of amusement with his seemingly effortless and virile charm.

New Yorker

Connery remains watchable, as always, but these are not two of his better hours.

TOD MCARTHY *Variety*

Sean Connery in
Medicine Man.

HONOURS, AWARDS AND TRUST

1965   Variety Club of Great Britain
       Silver Heart: Film Actor of the Year
1966   David di Donatello Prize, Italy
       Special Plaque: Actor
1971   Sean Connery founded the Scottish International Education Trust (SIET)
1971   Hollywood Foreign Press Association
       Golden Globe: World Film Favourite
1976   David di Donatello Prize, Italy
       Special Plaque: Actor
1981   Hon.D.Litt. Heriot-Watt University, Scotland
1983   Retrospective Season at the National Film Theatre, London
1984   Fellow of the Royal Scottish Academy of Music and Drama
1984   Harvard University, USA
       Man of the Year
1987   Commandeur des Arts et des Lettres, France
1987   British Film Critics' Circle
       Acting: *The Untouchables* and *The Name of the Rose*
1987   British Academy of Film and Television Arts (BAFTA)
       Best Actor: *The Name of the Rose*
1987   Federal Republic of Germany Film Prize
       Acting: *The Name of the Rose*
1987   D. W. Griffith Award, USA
       Best Supporting Actor: *The Untouchables*
1987   The American Academy of Motion Picture Arts and Sciences
       Oscar for Best Supporting Actor: *The Untouchables*
1987   Hollywood Foreign Press Association
       Golden Globe Best Supporting Actor: *The Untouchables*
1988   Hon.D.Litt. St Andrews University
1989   Variety Club of Great Britain
       Silver Heart: Film Actor of the Year
1990   British Academy of Film and Television Arts (BAFTA)
       Tribute Award: given to the British actor who has made an outstanding
       contribution to world cinema
1990   Man of Culture, Rome
1991   The Freedom of the City, Edinburgh
1991   Légion d'Honneur, France
1991   BBC Scotland
       Scot of the Year
1992   American Cinemateque Award
1992   Rudolph Valentino Award

CHRONOLOGY

FILM

Date	Title	Role	Screenplay	Director
1956	No Road Back	Spike	Charles A. Leeds and Montgomery Tully, additional dialogue by Falkland L. Cary and Philip Weathers, from *Madame Tic Tac,* a play by Falkland L. Cary and Philip Weathers	Montgomery Tully
1957	Hell Drivers	Johnny	John Kruse and C. Raker Endfield	C. Raker Endfield
	Time Lock	Second Welder	Peter Rogers from the play by Arthur Hailey	Gerald Thomas
	Action of the Tiger	Mike	Robert Carson based on the novel *Action of the Tiger* by James Wellard, adapted for the screen by Peter Myers	Terence Young
1958	Another Time, Another Place	Mark Trevor	Stanley Mann based on the novel by Leonore Coffee	Lewis Allen
1959	Darby O'Gill and the Little People	Michael McBride	Lawrence Edward Watkin suggested by H.T. Kavanagh's Darby O'Gill stories	Robert Stevenson
	Tarzan's Greatest Adventure	O'Bannion	Berne Giler and John Guillermin from a story by Les Crutchfield, based upon characters created by Edgar Rice Burroughs	John Guillermin
1961	The Frightened City	Paddy Damion	Leigh Vance, original story by Leigh Vance and John Lemont	John Lemont
	On the Fiddle (US titles: Operation Snafu Operation Warhead)	Pedlar Pascoe	Harold Buchman from the novel *Stop at a Winner* by R.F. Delderfield	Cyril Frankel
1962	The Longest Day	Pte Flanagan	Cornelius Ryan based on his own book, additional episodes written by Romain Gary, James Jones, David Pascall and Jack Seddon	Darryl F. Zanuck, Andrew Marton, Ken Annakin, Bernhard Wicki
	Dr. No	James Bond	Richard Maibaum, Johanna Harwood and Berkely Mather based on the novel by Ian Fleming	Terence Young
1963	From Russia With Love	James Bond	Richard Maibaum and Johanna Harwood based on the novel by Ian Fleming	Terence Young
1964	Woman of Straw	Anthony Richmond	Robert Muller, Stanley Mann and Michael Relph from the novel by Catherine Arley	Basil Dearden
	Marnie	Mark Rutland	Jay Presson Allen from the novel by Winston Graham	Alfred Hitchcock
	Goldfinger	James Bond	Richard Maibaum and Paul Dehn based on the novel by Ian Fleming	Guy Hamilton
1965	The Hill	Joe Roberts	Ray Rigby based on the original play by Ray Rigby and R.S. Allen	Sidney Lumet

1965	Thunderball	James Bond	Richard Maibaum and John Hopkins from an original story by Kevin McClory, Jack Whittingham and Ian Fleming, based on Ian Fleming's novel	Terence Young
1966	A Fine Madness	Samson Shillitoe	Elliott Baker based upon his novel	Irvin Kershner
1967	You Only Live Twice	James Bond	Roald Dahl based on the novel by Ian Fleming with additional story material by Harry Jack Bloom	Lewis Gilbert
1968	Shalako	Shalako	J.J. Griffith, Hal Hopper and Scot Finch from the screen story by Clarke Reynolds, based on a novel by Louis L'Amour	Edward Dmytryk
1969	The Molly Maguires	Jack Kehoe	Walter Bernstein suggested by a book by Arthur H. Lewis	Martin Ritt
	La Tenda Rossa (English title: The Red Tent)	Amundsen	Ennio de Concini and Richard Adams	Mikhail Kalatozov
1971	The Anderson Tapes	Duke Anderson	Frank R. Pierson based on the novel *The Anderson Tapes* by Lawrence Sanders	Sidney Lumet
	Diamonds Are Forever	James Bond	Richard Maibaum and Tom Mankiewicz based on the novel by Ian Fleming	Guy Hamilton
1972	The Offence	Johnson	John Hopkins based on his play *This Story of Yours*	Sidney Lumet
1973	Zardoz	Zed	John Boorman, story associate Bill Stair	John Boorman
1974	Ransom (US title: The Terrorists)	Nils Tahlvik	Paul Wheeler	Casper Wrede
	Murder on the Orient Express	Colonel Arbuthnot	Paul Dehn based on the novel by Agatha Christie	Sidney Lumet
1975	The Wind and the Lion	Raisuli	John Milius	John Milius
	The Man Who Would Be King	Daniel Dravot	John Huston and Gladys Hill from the Rudyard Kipling story	John Huston
1976	Robin and Marian	Robin Hood	James Goldman	Richard Lester
	The Next Man	Khalil Abdul-Muhsen	Mort Fine, Alan R. Trustman, David M. Wolf, Richard C. Sarafian, story by Alan R. Trustman and David M. Wolf	Richard C. Sarafian
1977	A Bridge Too Far	Major-General Urquhart	William Goldman from the book by Cornelius Ryan	Richard Attenborough
1978	The First Great Train Robbery (US title: The Great Train Robbery)	Edward Pierce	Michael Crichton based on his novel *The Great Train Robbery*	Michael Crichton
1979	Meteor	Dr Paul Bradley	Stanley Mann and Edmund H. North, story by Edmund H. North	Ronald Neame
	Cuba	Major Robert Dapes	Charles Wood	Richard Lester
1981	Time Bandits	King Agamemnon	Michael Palin and Terry Gilliam	Terry Gilliam

1981	Outland	Marshal O'Neil	Peter Hyams	Peter Hyams
1982	The Man With The Deadly Lens (US title: Wrong Is Right)	Patrick Hale	Richard Brooks based on the novel *The Better Angels* by Charles McCarry	Richard Brooks
	Five Days One Summer	Douglas	Michael Austin based in part on a short story *Maiden Maiden* by Kate Boyle	Fred Zinnemann
1983	Sword of the Valiant – The Legend of Gawain and the Green Knight	Green Knight	Stephen Weeks, Howard C. Pen and Philip M. Breen	Stephen Weeks
	G'Ole	Narrator	Stan Hey	Tom Clegg
	Never Say Never Again	James Bond	Lorenzo Semple Jr.	Irvin Kershner
1986	Highlander	Ramirez	Gregory Widen, Peter Bellwood and Larry Ferguson, story Gregory Widen	Russell Mulcahy
	Der Name der Rose (English title: The Name of The Rose)	William of Baskerville	Andrew Birkin, Gerard Brach, Howard Franklin, Alain Godard based on the novel by Umberto Eco	Jean-Jacques Annaud
1987	The Untouchables	Jim Malone	David Mamet, suggested by the television series and based on the works by Oscar Fraley with Eliot Ness and with Paul Robsky	Brian de Palma
1988	The Presidio	Lt.-Col. Alan Caldwell	Larry Ferguson	Peter Hyams
	Memories of Me	Himself	Billy Crystal and Alan King	Henry Winkler
1989	Indiana Jones and the Last Crusade	Professor Henry Jones	Jeffrey Boam, story by George Lucas and Menno Meyjes based on characters created by George Lucas and Philip Kaufman	Steven Spielberg
	Family Business	Jessie McMullen	Vincent Patrick based upon his novel	Sidney Lumet
1990	The Hunt for Red October	Markus Raimus	Larry Ferguson and Donald Stewart based on the novel by Tom Clancy	John McTiernan
	The Russia House	Barley Blair	Tom Stoppard based on the novel by John le Carré	Fred Schepisi
1991	Highlander II – The Quickening	Ramirez	Peter Bellwood, story by Brian Clemens and William Panzer	Russell Mulcahy
	Robin Hood – Prince of Thieves	Richard I	Pen Densham and John Watson, story by Pen Densham	Kevin Costner
1992	Medicine Man	Dr Robert Campbell	Tom Schulman, story by Tom Schulman and Sally Robinson	John McTiernan

THEATRE

Date	Play	Role	Author	Director	Theatre
1953	Sixty Glorious Years	guardsman	book Robert Nesbitt, music Harry Parr Davies, lyrics Harold Purcell	Robert Nesbitt	Empire, Edinburgh
	South Pacific	chorus Buzz Adams	book Oscar Hammerstein II and Joshua Logan, music Richard Rodgers, lyrics Oscar Hammerstein II	Joshua Logan	tour
1955	Witness for the Prosecution	court usher	Agatha Christie	Robert Henderson	Q
	Point of Departure	Mathias	Jean Anouilh, translated by Kitty Black	Frederick Farley	Q
	A Witch in Time	Robert Callender	Dolph Norman	Robert Henderson	Q
1956	The Good Sailor	O'Daniel	Louis O. Coxe and Robert Chapman based on the novel *Billy Budd* by Herman Melville	Frith Banbury	Lyric, Hammersmith
1959	The Bacchae	Pentheus	Euripides, translated by Minos Volanakis	Minos Volanakis	Playhouse, Oxford
	The Sea Shell	Frank Kittridge	Jess Gregg	Henry Kaplan	tour
1960	Anna Christie	Mat Burke	Eugene O'Neill	Douglas Seale	Playhouse, Oxford
	Naked	Consul Grotti	Luigi Pirandello, translated by Simon Nedia	Minos Volanakis	Playhouse, Oxford
1962	Judith	Holofernes	Jean Giraudoux, adapted by Christopher Fry	Harold Clurman	Her Majesty's
1969	I've Seen You Cut Lemons	(director only)	Ted Allan Herman	Sean Connery	Fortune

TELEVISION (Major Productions)

Date	Title	Role	Author	Director	Company
1957	Requiem for a Heavyweight	Mountain McClintock	Rod Serling	Alvin Rakoff	BBC
	Anna Christie	Mat Burke	Eugene O'Neill, adapted by Philip Saville	Philip Saville	ATV
1958	Women in Love (episode The Return)	Johnnie	Michael Ashe from a story by Kenneth Hyde	Robert Tronson	Associated Rediffusion
1959	The Square Ring	Rick Martell	Ralph W. Peterson, adapted by Jessica Morton	Bill Hitchcock	Associated Rediffusion
	The Crucible	John Proctor	Arthur Miller	Henry Kaplan	Associated Rediffusion
1960	Colombe (US title: Mademoiselle Colombe)	Julien	Jean Anouilh, translated and adapted by Denis Cannan	Naomi Capon	ATV
	An Age of Kings	Hotspur	William Shakespeare	Michael Hayes	BBC
	Without the Grail	Innes Corrie	Giles Cooper	Donald McWhinnie	BBC
	Riders to the Sea	Bartley	J.M. Synge	George R. Foa	BBC
	The Pets	Peter Connolly	Robert Shaw, an adaptation of his novel *The Hiding Place*	Peter Wood	Associated Rediffusion
	Macbeth	Macbeth	William Shakespeare		Canada
1961	Adventure Story	Alexander the Great	Terence Rattigan	Rudolph Cartier	BBC
	Anna Karenina	Vronsky	Marcelle-Maurette's version of the Leo Tolstoy novel, translated by E.J. King, adapted by Donald Bull	Rudolph Cartier	BBC
1967	Castles of Scotland	Narrator	Documentary	Austin Campbell	Scottish
	The Bowler and The Bunnet	Narrator	Sean Connery (documentary)	Sean Connery	Scottish
1969	MacNeil (US title: Male of the Species)	MacNeil	Alun Owen	Charles Jarrot	ATV
1982	Sean Connery's Edinburgh	Narrator	Sean Connery (documentary)	Sean Connery	Scottish

RADIO

Date	Title	Role	Author	Director	Company
1986	After the Funeral	Blair	Peter Barnes	Ian Cotterell	Radio 3

RECORDINGS

Date	Title	Role	Composer	Conductor	Company
1959	Pretty Irish Girl	Singer	Oliver Wallace and Lawrence Edward Watkin		Top Rank
	Ballamaquilty's Band	Singer	traditional		Top Rank
1966	Peter and the Wolf	Narrator	Sergey Prokofiev	Antal Dorati	Decca

ACKNOWLEDGEMENTS

The author would like to begin by thanking Ian and Marjory Chapman, Greg Hill, his editor Julia Martin and his designer Judy Linard.

The author and publisher would like to express their appreciation to the following for their assistance and/or permission in relation to the following photographs:

Anglo-Amalgamated 34, 35, 37; Artists Entertainment Complex 123, 124; Cannon 149; Columbia Pictures Corporation 12, 108, 110, 114, 143, 144; Columbia/Lastar 118, 120, 122; EMI 106, 153, 154, 181; Granada 30; Guild 183; HandMade Films 138, 139; Kingston 82, 83; Lion International 104, 105; Lucas/UIP 15, 166, 168, 169; Metro-Goldwyn-Mayer Seven Arts 23, 63, 64, 66; The National Film Archive London 12, 15, 18, 20, 22, 23, 24, 25, 26, 29, 37, 41, 42, 45, 46, 47, 49, 50, 52, 53, 54, 56, 57, 58, 61, 63, 64, 66, 68, 71, 72, 73, 74, 75, 76, 78, 79, 83, 84, 88, 89, 95, 96, 99, 102, 103, 104, 105, 106, 108, 110, 114, 122, 123, 124, 134, 138, 139, 141, 147, 148, 149, 152, 154, 160, 164, 166, 168, 169, 171, 174, 176, 181, 185; Neue Constantin Film Produktion 2, 157, 158; Palace Pictures 170, 171, 172; Palladium 132; Paramount Pictures Corporation 24, 25, 29, 90, 137, 160, 162, 163, 174, 175, 176; Paramount Pictures Corporation and Tamm Productions 84, 86, 88, 89; Pathé Entertainment Inc 173, 179, 180; The Rank Organisation plc 20; Romulus 22; Studio Edmark Oxford 28, 32, 33; The Times Newspapers Ltd 7, 19, 44, 48, 50, 62, 80, 91, 93, 94, 112, 113, 115, 116, 165, 177; Twentieth Century-Fox 41, 100, 102, 103; United Artists Corporation 127, 128, 129, 130, 131, 134, 136; United Artists/Eon 42, 45, 46, 47, 49, 58, 60, 61, 67, 68, 70, 71, 75, 76, 78, 79, 95; United Artists/Novus 52, 53; United Artists/Tantallon 96, 98, 99; Universal International Pictures 54, 56, 57, 164, 165; Walt Disney 26; Warner/Ladd 140, 141, 142, 147, 148; Warner Seven Arts 72, 73, 74; Warner/Woodcote 150, 152.

The author would also like to add a personal note of thanks to Don Baker, Judith Barnes, Sally Dean, Peter Hirst, Maha Kingman, Alfred Lynch, Anna Quayle, M. Roffey, staff at the Theatre Museum, and everybody at the BFI reference library, stills and viewing service.

INDEX